Markets, Morals and Development

This book presents, or rather "re-presents", the intricacies of a developing economy in the light of recent theoretical developments in economics while also providing a fresh perspective on the perceived inadequacies of the discipline in addressing the discontents of the contemporary global economic order.

The book argues that there is scope for economics to be a more humane discipline and more relevant to contemporary economic problems by embracing new ideas, including those from other disciplines. It attempts to show how economic concepts and theories can be contextualised to help better understand real-life economic phenomena; how to rethink the ways in which the market economy can address the moral issues of human well-being and social justice; and, overall, how the study of economics and public discourses on economic issues can be made more engaging as well as more relevant to the problems of developing countries. Based on public lectures given by the author in Dhaka, and using illustrations from Bangladesh, India and other countries, the book offers an authoritative understanding of diverse economic realities by taking a fresh look at the familiar.

Comprehensive and accessible, the book will be of interest to students and researchers of economics, development economics and policy, sociology and business studies as well as to journalists, public intellectuals and policymakers in developing countries.

Wahiduddin Mahmud (PhD in economics, University of Cambridge) is a former Professor of Economics at the University of Dhaka and is currently Chairman, Economic Research Group, Dhaka. He is also affiliated with International Growth Centre at the London School of Economics and is on the Board of the Global Development Network. He was a member of the UN Committee for Development Policy and has held visiting research positions at the World Bank, UN Development Programme (UNDP), International Food Policy Research Institute (IFPRI) and Institute of Development Studies at the University of Sussex. He was a member of the caretaker government of Bangladesh in charge of the ministries of finance and planning.

"At the same time short and sweeping, this book by Wahiduddin Mahmud is a remarkable survey and critique of modern economics. What makes the book special is the author's novel perspective which allows for the possibility of breaking tradition and writing a full description of economics using the developing country as a template, since such countries capture a broader canvas of life, from the informal *bazaars* to modern malls and financial markets. With allusions to literature, psychology and anthropology, and sprinkled with illustrations from Bangladesh, India and other economies, Mahmud's book is a pleasure to read."

—Kaushik Basu, Professor of Economics and Carl Marks Professor of International Studies, Cornell University

Markets, Morals and Development

Rethinking Economics from a
Developing Country Perspective

Wahiduddin Mahmud

Routledge
Taylor & Francis Group

LONDON AND NEW YORK

First published 2022
by Routledge
2 Park Square, Milton Park, Abingdon, Oxon OX14 4RN

and by Routledge
605 Third Avenue, New York, NY 10158

Routledge is an imprint of the Taylor & Francis Group, an informa business

© 2022 Wahiduddin Mahmud

The right of Wahiduddin Mahmud to be identified as authors of this work
has been asserted in accordance with sections 77 and 78 of the Copyright,
Designs and Patents Act 1988.

British Library Cataloguing-in-Publication Data
A catalogue record for this book is available from the British Library

Library of Congress Cataloging-in-Publication Data
A catalog record has been requested for this book

ISBN: 978-1-032-11682-2 (hbk)
ISBN: 978-1-032-14924-0 (pbk)
ISBN: 978-1-003-24177-5 (ebk)

DOI: 10.4324/9781003241775

Typeset in Times New Roman
by Deanta Global Publishing Services, Chennai, India

To
Adeeb and Shamarukh
Naved and Jennifer
Ayesha, Joseph and Samir

Contents

Acknowledgements

The book originates from a series of public lectures I gave during 2016–2021, organised by Brac University and North South University in Dhaka, Shahjalal University of Science and Technology in Sylhet and *Banglar Pathsala*, a study circle in Dhaka. I am grateful to the organisers of those lectures.

I am deeply indebted to Salim Rashid, Professor Emeritus of Economics at the University of Illinois Urbana-Champaign, for painstakingly reading the entire draft manuscript and providing detailed comments and suggestions for improving the articulation of arguments, arrangement of the materials and the overall readability of the book. I also thank Professor Syed M. Ahsan of Concordia University and Professor M. G. Quibria of Morgan State University for making valuable comments on the manuscript. Interactions with my former students and colleagues at the University of Dhaka – some of them well-established academics worldwide – have helped me to develop the ideas contained in this book. The book also draws on materials from some occasional lectures I gave during the 2000s at Yale University, mostly at the invitation of late Professor T. N. Srinivasan for his South Asia seminar course. I am grateful to Professor Amartya Sen for commenting on my keynote presentation at a workshop on his works held in Dhaka in March 2021. Needless to say, I alone am responsible for any errors and shortcomings of the book.

For permissions to reuse two of my published journal papers in Chapters 5 and 6, I am grateful to the respective copyright owners:

Mahmud, W. "Socio-economic progress with poor governance: How are Amartya Sen's thoughts relevant for contemporary Bangladesh", *Indian Journal of Human Development*, Vol. 14, Number 3, December 2020, pp. 359–71. © 2020 Institute for Human Development. Reprinted by permission of SAGE Publications India Private Limited. https://doi.org/10.1177%2F0973703020968475;

Mahmud, W. "Is there an economics of social business?", *The Bangladesh Development Studies*, Vol. XXXXB, Sept.–Dec. 2017, Numbers 3 & 4, pp.159–69. © 2020 Bangladesh Institute of Development Studies.

Wahiduddin Mahmud

1   Introduction

Economics was once called "the dismal science" by Thomas Carlyle, an eighteenth-century Scottish writer and philosopher. Although the exact context of his using the phrase remains somewhat mythical, he was referring to the dire predictions made by the economists of his time, especially Thomas Malthus, about humanity trapped in a world of widespread misery and impoverishment. Today, when we hear the term "the dismal science", it is typically in reference to the inadequacies of the discipline in addressing the discontents of the contemporary global economic order with its supremacy of the market – an economic order that is characterised by instability and unprecedented inequality amidst plenty. While the market economy has become the dominant model for our societies, it is regarded with widespread distrust, mixed with outrage or fatalism. The less developed countries feel all the more aggrieved because of the perceived unfairness of the global market system that is tilted against their interest due to their relative lack of power vis-à-vis the industrialised North. Economics is derided, rightly or wrongly, for seeming to lend legitimacy to this market system that lacks compassion and is prey to private corporate interest.

There is also a growing apathy towards economics among students because of a disconnect they feel between textbook economics and the real-life economic phenomena that they observe in their surroundings. Although economics is in large part the study of markets, the textbooks depict them abstractly and do not often provide enough guidance in understanding how markets may fail or thrive under various socio-cultural environments. While such an understanding of the functioning of the markets is of particular interest to the students in the less developed countries, they may feel frustrated by the fact that there is no developing country equivalent of Paul Samuelson's *Economics: An Introductory Analysis* (1948), which is arguably the best-known textbook on introductory economics ever written. With its 19 editions, the book is replete with examples ranging from the US families, firms, labour unions and government activities to

DOI: 10.4324/9781003241775-1

even the racial issues in that country. For the developing country students, this is certainly not the ideal way of relating textbook economics to real-life experience.

Yet, economics students in the developing countries have one advantage; they have the opportunity of applying the textbook market model to the actual functioning of markets in a whole range of institutional settings, from rural *hats* and *bazaars* to modern shopping malls. In the countless ways that they encounter economic dealings in their surroundings, there are always new insights to be gained from such dealings, if only they could take a fresh angle on the familiar. They may take heart from the fact that some of the recent theoretical advances in economics not only have deep practical content but also originated from observing markets in the less developed countries. For example, George Akerlof and Joseph Stiglitz both won the 2001 Nobel Prize in economics (along with Michael Spence) for laying the foundation of what is now called the theory of markets with imperfect information; of them, Stiglitz got his idea from the rural credit markets in South Asia and Akerlof's theory is especially applicable in explaining why adulterated food items pervade markets in less developed countries, such as the market for fresh milk in the *bazaars* of Delhi and Dhaka (as discussed in Chapter 2 of this book). There may be more such ingredients or hidden gems in the institutions of markets in less developed countries that may potentially enrich our understanding of how markets can work better in some environments than in others and how well-functioning markets can be a vehicle for achieving economic development.

There may also be a growing apathy among policymakers in the less developed countries towards policy advice coming from academic economists in the West, often through the intermediation of the international financial institutions. Knowledge in development policy analysis, as in economics and other disciplines generally, originates from the rich-country institutions, with the academics in the elite institutions there playing the agenda-setting and gatekeeping role. This may create a mismatch between what is academically rewarding within those institutional cultures and what the policymakers in the Global South may actually need for practical purposes. For example, the Nobel Prize in economics in 2019 was awarded to Abhijit Banerjee, Esther Duflo and Michael Kremer for their pioneering experimental approach to impact evaluation, particularly in the case of interventions for poverty alleviation in developing countries. While this approach is now considered by many in the profession as the "gold standard" in terms of methodology, development practitioners may find it frustrating that such experiments, known in the literature as randomised control trials, are often not amenable to scaling up or that the research results may be of little relevance for devising policies that are not trivial.

The above concerns about the study and practice of economics are highlighted in the four chapters in this book. The chapters are the outcome of the public lectures the author gave in Dhaka during 2016–20 to an audience comprising of university students and young faculty of the economics departments and business schools as well as economic journalists and public intellectuals.

The lectures represent an attempt to demonstrate in an engaging way the ever-relevant and fascinating nature of economics – how the concepts and toolkits of economics, when applied with imagination, can help one to better understand real-life economic phenomena, often with a fresh and insightful perspective. There is also an attempt to show that, in spite of the alleged lack of compassion and empathy in economics as a discipline, there is ample scope to rethink the ways in which the market economy can address the moral issues of human well-being and social justice. Overall, the chapters attempt to show, with real-life examples, how the study of economics and public discourses on economic issues can be made more accessible and engaging as well as more relevant from the perspective of the less developed countries. While there are threads of common or related themes woven into the chapters, the overlaps have been kept to the minimum in collating the original lectures into a book format.

The first chapter (Chapter 2) examines how economists are trained to look at economic issues differently than others. By using examples, it discusses the distinctive perspectives that can be gained from economic concepts such as *counterfactuals, sunk cost* or *comparative* vis-à-vis *absolute* advantage; it also illustrates how using the logic derived from abstract economic models can help clarify issues, identify causal relationships and avoid arguments at cross-purposes in public discourses. The chapter argues that, in spite of the attempts at grand narratives through universally applicable theoretical constructs, useful economics is necessarily eclectic, so that the students of economics in developing countries have much to gain by trying to relate textbook theories to their own socio-cultural settings. This is illustrated by discussing the characteristics of some typical market institutions in the less developed countries.

For example, the cobweb-type demand–supply model used in the textbook for explaining high annual price fluctuations in agricultural markets is shown to be more applicable in the case of high-value minor crops than for staple food crops. Other examples show why it may be wrong to blame businessmen on ethical grounds for price hikes of certain food items at times of religious festivity, while the moral responsibility must also partly lie with the relatively wealthy buyers who may choose to apply some moderation in consuming the items in limited supply relative to demand, or how in the seasonal markets for fresh fruits, the consumers end up buying fruits artificially ripened by harmful chemicals while the "invisible hand" of the market works through the self-seeking behaviour of thieves, fruit farmers, freight handlers and traders, albeit in an environment of lax law enforcement.

While some of the recent theoretical advances in economics, such as the theory of market with imperfect information, are of particular practical relevance for the less developed countries, knowledge of ground realities can provide further insights into the application of these theories. For example, Joseph Stiglitz formulated his theory of rural credit markets on the assumption that a poor borrower of a collateral-free business loan may use the loan inefficiently, such as by going for more profitable but riskier projects, since the risk of the failure of the business is borne by the lender (known in theory as the "ex ante moral hazard" problem). Stiglitz further theorised how the introduction of the Grameen Bank's microcredit programme in Bangladesh sought to solve this problem through a system of group lending; the members of the group monitored one another's use of loan because of the joint-liability for loan repayment.

While Stiglitz's above theory has become part of textbook economics, the underlying logic of moral hazard – the key point of his theory – may not apply anymore to a mature microfinance system such as in Bangladesh, which has almost dispensed with joint-liability group lending. Because of the well-established culture of loan repayment and the social stigma attached to being branded as a defaulter, the cost of non-repayment in the mental calculation of the borrower can be high enough to ensure that she is not contemplating non-repayment regardless of the anticipated success or failure of her business – hence no moral hazard arising from the asymmetry of interest between the lender and the borrower. Ironically, while Stiglitz was theorising the problem of providing credit to the rural poor, the logic of his theory may apply more to the formal banking system in many less developed countries with poor enforcement of loan recovery. This also provides an example of how academic theorising about development policies may not always keep pace with the ground-level institutional innovations taking place through a learning-by-doing process.

The purpose of the second chapter (Chapter 3) is to review and rethink how and to what extent ethical considerations and the precepts of moral philosophy affect the theory and application of economics. In pursuing purely "objective" analyses and, thereby, attaining the status of science, neoclassical economic theory is constrained by self-imposed limitations in making value judgements about justice and fairness in a market economy. Adam Smith's idea of the "invisible hand" guiding the market through self-interested behaviour has sometimes been interpreted, wrongly, as a kind of market fundamentalism that ignores many failures and brutalities of modern-day capitalism. While many ethical elements do go into economic policy analyses, these are still constrained by the discipline's relative neglect of non-market activities and its tendency to undervalue the aspects of well-being which cannot be easily measured in monetary terms.

The chapter argues that economists may do better by improving their understanding of the complexity of human behaviour, for example, by drawing from new ideas developed in neuroscience and experimental psychology; they also need to allow more scope for ethical judgements in their choice of topics for inquiry, in their methodological approaches and in drawing policy conclusions. Even if the motivation for monetary gains may be the dominant behavioural trait in economic dealings, there are instances in which the separation of self-interest from other traits including ethical values is less than straightforward. Deep moral questions may also arise regarding the fairness or welfare-enhancing role of free market transactions between parties of unequal economic power, such as between the rich and the poor countries or between a landlord and his tenants in a peasant economy.

The third chapter (Chapter 4) discusses the broader theme of how economic development is accompanied by a process of institutional transformation in which traditional production technologies, local knowledge and informal behavioural norms are replaced or complemented by improved technologies, modern know-how and formal regulatory enforcement of business dealings. Of particular interest is how social norms of trust, reciprocity and cooperation evolve in ways not easily explained by the pursuit of self-interest only. Economists may prefer the so-called "Prisoner's Dilemma"-type explanation of learning the benefit of cooperation from the experience of repeated interaction, while individualistic selfish behaviour may be the dominant strategy to start with. Other social scientists may prefer to find explanations in human traits like altruism, instinct, trust and various community-specific characteristics; some may even look for the historical roots of cooperative behaviour in the agricultural irrigation systems. It is argued that, whatever may be the historical origins of the social institutions and behavioural norms, these should be taken into account through community involvement in designing local development programmes; otherwise, such programmes may not yield the desired outcomes and may even be counterproductive.

The chapter also suggests that an understanding of how common values and ethical norms underlying the functioning of markets evolve may give economists better clues and insights in making policy analyses for economic development. In the contemporary literature on economic development, there is a new emphasis on "governance", originating mostly from the Bretton Woods institutions; the usual policy advice is mainly to do with devising and enforcing appropriate administrative policy reforms and enforcing regulatory laws aimed at building market-friendly institutions. Such a technocratic approach to reforms, it is argued, is unlikely to succeed without an understanding of how incentives for deviant behaviour arise and how legal and regulatory enforcement mechanisms interact with the evolution of behavioural norms and moral standards in a society.

The fourth chapter (Chapter 5) discusses the ideas of Nobel laureate economist Amartya Sen in the context of understanding the socio-economic progress achieved in Bangladesh and the challenges that lie ahead. Sen is one of the great economist-philosophers of the contemporary world, and the overriding concerns in his writings are about how to promote public action towards achieving an equitable and just society, which particularly addresses the needs of the underprivileged. While his ideas are of great relevance for all developing countries, this is more so for India and Bangladesh – the two countries that provide the socio-economic settings for much of his empirical works. Sen has praised the remarkable progress in many social development indicators that Bangladesh has achieved compared to India, despite having a much lower per capita income and suffering from the same, or even much worse, institutional and policy failures. The case study of Bangladesh is of particular interest to test some of Sen's ideas, such as regarding famines, pathways of human development and the democratic space for what he calls "public reasoning". By applying Sen's ideas for understanding Bangladesh's socio-economic progress, the chapter also examines the relevance of these ideas in the varying socio-political settings across developing countries.

The fifth and final chapter (Chapter 6) looks at how the idea of socially oriented business enterprises can be made conceptually compatible with the mainstream theory and practice of economics, and it also examines the potential of such experiments to be a moderating force against the excesses committed by the purely profit-motivated market economy. Within the broad genre of socially oriented enterprises, the chapter particularly focuses on the so-called "social business", as advocated by Nobel Peace laureate Muhammad Yunus. His idea of social business has drawn considerable attention from the global business community and many business schools around the world, but curiously, there has been little response so far from the mainstream economic profession. The chapter explores the reasons for this apathy and the ways in which the concept of social business, and socially oriented enterprises generally, could be reconciled with economic theorising. It also argues that a rigid definition of social business may leave a grey area in between such businesses and the purely profit-motivated ones, particularly since the "social" element may exist in various shades in the running of a business. Although the chapter primarily looks at the analytical aspects of the concept of social business, it does examine some of the risks and pitfalls involved in the actual implementation of such a business idea.

2 Thinking like an economist

Introduction: the study and practice of economics

Maynard Keynes once said that economics is a difficult subject, but nobody will believe it; it seems an easy subject compared to the high branches of philosophy or pure science, yet very few excel in it. In his view, the paradox may perhaps be explained by the fact that a good economist must possess a rare combination of gifts: he must be a mathematician, historian, statesman and philosopher in some degree. He needs the analytical mind "to contemplate the particular in terms of the general", and he has to be at the same time "as aloof and incorruptible as an artist, and yet as near the earth as a politician".[1] That is a tall order of things, and if it is true, it may be worth pondering over how economists view things and approach a problem differently than others.

The above view of Keynes suggests that useful economics is necessarily eclectic and that economic issues may be deceivingly complex. In spite of elegant theoretical constructs, such as the neoclassical general equilibrium theory, economists have increasingly come to realise that there are no grand narratives or universal theories of such generality as the laws of science. This is also how Alfred Marshall, known as the founder of neoclassical economics, approached economic theorising by emphasising the need for deductive logic, while also asserting: "I do not assign any universality to economic dogmas" (Pigou 1925, p. 89). Maynard Keynes interpreted this approach by saying that Marshall employed "deductive political economy guided by observation" (Keynes 1972, p. 164). Economic theories are thus best understood by trying to apply those to real-life situations. For example, the abstract lifeless demand–supply model of the market taught in introductory economics starts getting both exciting and complex when one tries to apply the model to explain the actual behaviour of various types of markets. In this respect, students in the developing countries have the advantage of applying the textbook theory to the functioning of markets in a whole

DOI: 10.4324/9781003241775-2

range of institutional settings that are familiar to them – from rural *hats* and *bazaars* to modern shopping malls. In the countless ways that they encounter economic dealings in their surroundings, there are always new insights to be gained from such dealings, if only they could take a fresh angle on the familiar.

The application of textbook economics to real-life situations has become more rewarding with the recent onslaught of new ideas into the theory and practice of mainstream economics, such as, with regard to markets with information asymmetry between buyers and sellers, environmental externalities, game-theoretic models of trust and cooperation leading to reinforcement of social norms, theories of individual behaviour derived from experimental psychology and the experimental approach to impact evaluation (randomised control trials). Many of these new ideas are not only appealing to the inquisitive mind but also more relevant in the context of less developed countries. Most of the modern theories of agrarian economics have also been developed from the perspectives of present-day less developed countries. The theoretical applications of some of these ideas can be found in the textbooks used in the courses on economic development at the graduate or advanced undergraduate levels,[2] but it should be possible to introduce these ideas in a more accessible way, both in introductory economics courses and in public discourses on economic issues.

Even if economic issues may be deceivingly complex, economists owe it to society to try to bridge the gap between the expert and the lay opinion on such issues. It is often frustrating for otherwise knowledgeable people to find debates on economic policies too technical and inaccessible, although the lives of everyone are affected by these policies. A do-it-yourself (DIY) approach to economics can easily lead to popular fallacies on economic issues. Yet, a minimum level of economic literacy among educated people is both possible and highly desirable. It is true that economists differ in their opinion on most economic issues and there are rarely ready-made unequivocal answers to questions commonly asked on such issues. This is a subject of many popular jokes, one of which is about a US president saying: I have ten economic advisors with ten different opinions; I know one of them is correct, but don't know which one. However, knowledgeable people need to know the basis of the different viewpoints without falling into the traps of economic fallacies, then make their own value judgements to reach their own conclusions.

Unfortunately, popularising serious policy debates on economic issues is not easy. As Nobel (2008) laureate economist Paul Krugman once lamented: Where is the economics equivalent of the late Carl Sagan who could make the technicalities of astrophysics accessible and exciting to a wide television audience? Later on, Krugman proved himself wrong; in

2000, he began a twice weekly op-ed column for *The New York Times*, and using this platform, he became America's most widely read commentator on political economy. Before that, Paul Samuelson, the twentieth-century titan of theoretical and mathematical economics, became one of the most familiar names to the numerous readers of *Newsweek, The New York Times* and the *Washington Post* where he wrote columns regularly for a decade and a half since the mid-1960s. These examples show that, instead of being boring and dry, serious discussions on economic issues may be interesting and engaging as well. As the novelist Mario Vargas Llosa remarked: "Economists occasionally tell better stories than novelists".[3] What he probably meant is that there are certainly rich ingredients in economic happenings to make engaging literary narratives; the stories of markets and businesses are full of human ingenuity and creativity, as well as disappointment and failure.

Economists are not, however, the favourites in any popularity contest, particularly since they have to carefully avoid playing to the gallery. Alfred Marshall warned economists long ago not to advocate opinions unconditionally and to "fear popular approval" (Pigou 1925, p. 89). To the passionate partisan and ideologically inclined readers, the commentaries by an economist may seem too ambivalent and non-committal for their taste. The refuting of popular economic fallacies is unlikely to go down well with those who would rather cling to their long-held beliefs. Economists may also be called upon to provide policy advice on unpalatable choices which other professions would rather avoid, like how to allocate resources in the government's health budget between the provision of universal primary health care and spending on costly intensive care in hospitals for the few who need such life-saving medical care. Nobel (2014) laureate economist Jean Tirole explains another reason why the public perception about the profession of economists is far less favourable than that of medicine, otherwise known as the "the caring profession". In medicine, the benefit of treatment goes directly to the patients, even when an infectious disease spreads in the community. In contrast, an economist's considered advice may involve conflicting interests of different groups of people; since he is obliged to think about the indirect victims of a policy, he may be accused of being indifferent to the interest of the direct beneficiaries of the policy (Tirole 2007, pp. 2–4).

On a lighter note, does thinking like an economist say anything about the economists' personal qualities? After all, in their academic work, they deal mainly with the self-regarding behaviour of people that could lead them to view the world through a distorted lens. Some studies in experimental psychology carried on university students do suggest that students who opt for economics tend to be less generous compared to students of other social science disciplines, but this may be more because of self-selection (students are more likely to major in economics or business if they are more selfish) than because of indoctrination (students become selfish because of studying economics).[4] In any case, beyond any short-term effect of studying economics, there is no research finding to show if economists in their later personal and professional life act less ethically than people in other professions. In the less developed countries, economists are in fact generally regarded as being especially compassionate in their role as public intellectuals, since they are inevitably called upon to discuss ways of poverty alleviation. Overall, given thus that there is no evidence of at least any long-term damage to ethical values from thinking like an economist, the non-economist readers of this chapter may feel reassured on this account to proceed further!

Looking for causality

Economic analyses primarily seek to find causal relationships between various economic variables, such as the impact on the market price of a change in the supply of a commodity, or the impact of a policy in achieving its intended goals. Economics contrasts with other social sciences in trying to establish such relationships in as much a precise or "scientific" way as possible. However, economic predictions have to be made in a world where everything depends on everything else, or at least a number of other things. By contrast, physicists can study a falling body in complete isolation from almost everything except gravity. A simplistic comparison of the situation prevailing *before* and *after* the implementation of an economic policy can be a misleading way of assessing the impact of that policy. The outcome of a policy reform can be ideally assessed only by looking at the *counterfactual*, that is, a *with-and-without* comparison by separating the effects of all other extraneous factors working simultaneously. This is by no means an easy task although economists have devised various statistical and methodological tools to do that with varying success. The logic of the counterfactual is not, however, always commonly understood, so it is often difficult to perceive that certain outcomes may have happened *in spite of* and not *because of* a policy.

Economic models

In understanding economic problems, starting with a highly abstract simplified version of the real-life situations – the so-called economic models – can often be much more helpful than gathering incoherent ideas from a vast amount of general reading. Even the elementary model of market equilibrium, represented by the familiar diagram of intersecting demand and supply curves, can go a long way in helping to avoid confusion about how certain policies may affect the working of markets. I often used to tease my first-year undergraduate students in the Introduction to Economics course with the following problem: the "law of demand" says that the demand for apple will increase if the price falls, but everybody will also agree that if the demand for apple increases, its price will increase. While both the statements sound very sensible, how is it that they also appear to be contradictory regarding the relative movements of price and demand? The answer to this puzzle, of course, lies in the hidden assumptions behind the two statements. The law of demand regarding the inverse relation between price and demand – represented by the downward-sloping demand curve – is derived from a deductive logic that we get decreasing extra satisfaction from an extra apple and will therefore demand more apple only if the price falls. It is a hypothetical relationship based on the assumption that other things except price, such as income, taste and prices of rival goods, remain the same. Underlying this logic behind the law of demand is the cardinal *marginalist* principle, which has been used to explain decision-making in neoclassical economics since Alfred Marshall's *Principles of Economics*. Unlike the proverbial pupil who did not quite know where to stop in spelling *banana...*, a rational individual will make a decision on the basis not of *total* but *marginal* or extra benefit and cost (in the above example, the extra satisfaction from one more apple compared to its price, that is, the extra cost).

The second statement is about the determination of price through the interaction of market demand and supply. When we say that the price of apple has increased because of an increase in demand, it has happened precisely because of a change in one or more of those other things except price that we assumed to remain unchanged in deriving the "law of demand". Thus, an increase in people's income will push the market demand for apple upward, which in turn will result in a price increase through the demand–supply interaction. In terms of the elementary demand–supply market model, the above two statements can easily be seen to relate, respectively, to a *movement along* a downward-sloping demand curve and to an upward *shift* of the demand curve resulting in an increase in the equilibrium market price.

Thinking in terms of an economic model often helps to make a precise statement without creating confusion; otherwise, unnecessary controversies may arise with people talking at cross-purposes. An example is provided by a rhetorical public debate back in 2014 between the Commerce Minister of Bangladesh, Mr. Tofail Ahmed, and the then US ambassador to Bangladesh, Mr. Dan Mozena, about who pays the burden of a 15 percent import tariff levied by the United States on Bangladesh's apparel export. Ambassador Mozena's contention was that the burden of this tariff was borne by the US consumers who buy the imported apparel, while Mr. Ahmed claimed that it was the Bangladeshi garment producers who had to pay the entire bill. In fact, both were right to an extent, but they were talking from different premises.

Ambassador Mozena was referring to the textbook case of the effect of high import tariffs, the burden of which is borne in part by the US consumers (but also in part by the exporting countries generally in terms of a lower price and a lower trade volume, the United States being a major importer in the global garment market), with Bangladesh not particularly discriminated against. Mr. Ahmed, on the other hand, was comparing the existing situation with a hypothetical one in which the United States would have offered an exclusive tax-free facility to Bangladeshi apparel exports, which he thought was deserved by Bangladesh because of its status of Least Developed Country. The impact of allowing such a tax concession on the US domestic apparel price would be marginal, if at all, because exports from Bangladesh constitute only a fraction of the US domestic apparel market (about 5 percent). Thus, compared to allowing such a tariff concession, the impact of the existing US import tariff can be said to fall largely, if not entirely, on the Bangladeshi exporters. When I wrote an op-ed explaining the cause of this controversy, T. N. Srinivasan, the late Yale University economist and an authority on the theory of international trade, sent me a diagrammatic exposition of my explanation – an example of how economists are rarely satisfied with an argument until it can be laid out in terms of a clearly defined model (Mahmud 2014).

In Figure 2.1, D is the domestic demand curve of imported garments in the US domestic market; S0 is the worldwide supply from exporters without

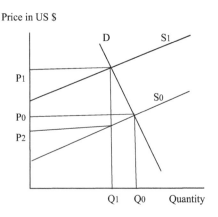

Figure 2.1 The impact of US import tariffs on garments exporters of Bangladesh.

any import duty and S1 is the supply curve with the existing duty. The supply curve shifts upward exactly by the amount of the duty, implying that the same quantity will be supplied at the original price plus the duty (the duty is assumed for simplicity to be at a fixed rate per unit of quantity, and not per unit value, that is, *ad valorem*). The US domestic price is P0 without tax and P1 with tax, while Q1 and Q0 are the quantities imported with and without duty, respectively.

Ambassador Mozena's argument: because of the duty, the increase in the price paid by the US domestic consumers is (P1 − P0), which is a large part of the unit duty rate of (P1 − P2), represented by the extent of the upward shift of the supply curve. It can be shown that this part of the duty borne by the US consumers depends on the relative slopes of the supply and demand curves. Minister Tofail Ahmed's argument: if Bangladeshi exports were exclusively given duty-free facility, these exports would get the price P1, instead of the price P2, the difference being exactly equal to the duty rate. Bangladesh is also likely to gain from exporting a higher quantity in response to the higher price, but that was not the point of contention.

The counterfactual vis-à-vis the actual

Coming back to the logic of the *counterfactual*, conceptualising it can be of varying complexities, depending on the ways in which the counterfactual is expected to be different from the actual. Consider, for example, the impact on the consumption and saving patterns of a household, an earning member of which temporarily migrates overseas to earn a better income and send remittances back to the family left behind. Several things will happen (besides the initial costs incurred for migration): first, there will be a change in the family income to the extent that the monthly or yearly remittance sent by the migrant worker exceeds the income he could have earned without migrating. Second, with the additional income, the remittance-receiving household is likely to spend their income differently compared to other households with similar income because there is one person less in the household to meet living expenses, but, more importantly, because the income from remittances is regarded to be of temporary and windfall nature as distinct from regular household income (Mahmud 1989).

One empirical method of estimating this impact of overseas migration is to conduct household surveys to gather relevant information on two groups of households, one with a migrant household member and another with none, and compare their income and spending patterns. Since the two groups of households may differ in ways other than having or not having a migrant member, econometric methods are used to "control" for the differences, but still the comparison may not be an ideal one because of the likelihood of "unobservable" differences that may exist between the two household groups. Better results may be obtained by conducting repeated surveys over a period of time on both groups of households, known as *longitudinal* surveys, and applying appropriate statistical techniques to the data so generated.

An even more statistically superior approach would be to conduct an experiment by sending abroad for overseas employment members of some randomly selected households from a larger group of households, each with a prospective migrant member, and subsequently comparing the situations of the two groups. The Nobel Prize in economics in 2019 was awarded to Abhijit Banerjee, Esther Duflo and Michael Kremer for pioneering this experimental approach, known as the randomised control trials, which is now considered by many in the profession as the "gold standard" of impact evaluation, particularly in the case of interventions for poverty alleviation in developing countries. While in terms of methodology, this experimental approach should be able to empirically capture the *counterfactual* as closely as possible, it has been critiqued for several reasons: the practical difficulties in finding an ideal experimental set up, particularly for policies that are not trivial; the validity of the results in other socio-economic settings, particularly when there are no *a priori* analytical framework of a causal relationship; and ethical issues involved in the random selection of the programme beneficiaries instead of prioritising those who are otherwise considered to be more deserving.

Though not often practised, there is yet another way of getting at the counterfactual in an empirical study based on field surveys; the survey questionnaire can be administered in a way that involves a mental exercise on the part of the respondent regarding the counterfactual. Consider, for example, an important question in evaluating the impact of microfinance on poor borrowers: How have the loans been utilised? Simply asking this question in a survey of borrowers may elicit misleading answers due to the fungibility of funds. For example, a particular expenditure such as to meet marriage expenses could have been incurred anyway irrespective of whether the loan was available or not, in which case the loan in question is not actually causing any *additional* expenditure but in effect may be substituting other sources of financing like asset sale, depletion of saving or borrowing from alternative sources. One could ask, instead, probing questions so as to engage the survey respondents in a mental exercise about the counterfactual, such as: Would you have made a particular spending if you had no access to microfinance, and in that case, how would you have financed it? Mahmud and Osmani (2017, pp. 216–20) show how such probing questions in a survey can provide useful insights about the use of microfinance even if it may not be the exact counterfactual.

Economic logic versus instinctive thinking

The logic of many economic concepts is not easily perceived by people not trained in economics, since such logic may be at odds with the instinctive or intuitive thinking of people. Biases in people's perception often give rise to popular economic fallacies, which policymakers should be aware of and try to dispel. The way an individual makes choices and judgements may also be influenced by such biases, which will be a deviation from the basic assumption made in the economic theory that individuals act *rationally*. The modern field of behavioural economics is helping economists to understand how instinctive and biased perceptions may make an individual act differently than would be expected in conventional economic analyses. Behavioural economists such as Daniel Kahneman, an economics Nobel (2002) laureate, describes intuitive thoughts as generated by a system of thinking which is "typically automatic, quick, effortless, associative, and often emotionally charged" and "generates involuntary impressions that come to mind spontaneously ... with little modifications from the reasoning system".[5]

Absolute and comparative advantage

An important example of popular misperception about an economic concept is that of "comparative advantage" used in the theory of international trade. The theory, originally formulated by David Ricardo, provides the logic of trade among countries in terms of a country having a *comparative* rather than an *absolute* advantage in producing a tradable good. The logic, which can be easily illustrated by numerical examples, may not seem obvious at a first glance. The *absolute* advantage Adam Smith talked about is simple and intuitive: it makes obvious sense for France to export wine to Scotland and import Scotch Whisky. *Comparative* advantage is more complicated. Ricardo introduced the notion in his 1817 book, *On the Principles of Political Economy and Taxation*; he demonstrated numerically that, even if Portugal is more productive than England in both cloth and wine, both countries can gain with a rise in the total output of both goods if England specialised in cloth and Portugal in wine. Since comparative advantage is a concept of *relative* costs of doing things, no country can have a comparative advantage of everything, and every country must have a comparative advantage in something.

Being once called upon by a mathematician, Stainslaw Ulam (who did not have a high opinion of social sciences), to name one social science proposition that was both true and not trivial, Samuelson nominated comparative advantage: that this idea is logically true can be shown by a few lines of mathematics, as anyone with an hour or two's training in economics will know, and "that it is not trivial is attested by the thousands of important and intelligent men who have never been able to grasp the doctrine for themselves or to believe it after it was explained to them" (Samuelson 1969). To be sure, as Samuelson further remarks, the term *comparative advantage* is widely used, but *absolute advantage* is what politicians or non-economist pundits will usually have in mind. Subsequent developments in the trade theory have tried to explain why the actual pattern of global trade in today's world is explained by many factors other than the original theory of comparative advantage, but the basic insight from the theory remains useful.

On a personal note, a friend of mine who used to teach economics at the South Asian University in Delhi was once asked by a student from Nepal: Why should India trade with Nepal since it can produce nearly everything more efficiently?[6] My professor friend answered the student with an example which is perhaps the easiest way to explain the concept of comparative advantage, albeit referring to the era before the advent of laptops and word processing. Suppose a professor is more efficient than his secretary in typing, and of course in doing research, but it will not obviously make much sense for him to devote his time away from doing research to share the work of typing with his secretary.

There are more complicated uses of the concept of comparative advantage which are even far more difficult for non-economists to comprehend. Bilateral trade agreements are often made on the basis of mutual lowering or elimination of tariff barriers. The gains from such agreements depend on the balance of two types of impact: the usual positive gains derived by the increased volume of trade between the countries through specialisation in producing tradable items according to their mutual comparative advantage (the so-called *trade creation*); against this, there is a possible economic loss because of diversion of imports from cheaper third-country source to the costlier partner country resulting from the withdrawal of import tariffs exclusively for the partner country (the so-called *trade diversion*). Before such a trade agreement is reached, negotiations are held between the two prospective partner countries regarding which items are to be kept out of the tariff-free status in order to retain continued protection to certain domestic industries. When a negotiating high-level trade delegation, usually consisting of the government high officials of the commerce or trade department along with delegates of various business bodies, all appear happy after "successfully" signing the deal, an economist should have reasons to feel apprehensive. The benefit of trade creation should make some businessmen happy because of the prospect of exporting more to the partner country while others are bound to feel unhappy because of increased competition from imports from the partner country. *Trade diversion* represents a loss to the country, but it may not have much impact in lowering protection provided to domestic industries (depending on the extent to which domestic prices of imports are affected by diverting a cheaper source of import from a third-country subject to tariffs to the costlier but tariff-free imports from the partner country). The absence of seriously aggrieved businessmen in enough numbers may thus suggest that the negotiated trade arrangement may not result in much beneficial trade creation compared to harmful trade diversion.

The concept of sunk cost

The concept of what economists call "sunk cost" is useful in making economic decisions in a variety of circumstances, particularly in implementing investment projects; it is a cost that has been already incurred irrespective of what decisions are taken for further action. Suppose, after already spending one-third of the estimated cost of a government development project, there is some rethinking done on the basis of some revised assessment about the benefit to be derived from the completed project. Assuming that there is no cost for dismantling the work already done, the decision regarding whether to proceed further with the project should *rationally* depend only on the estimated gain from the completed project vis-à-vis the further cost to be incurred; the spending already done, which is now a *sunk* cost, should have no role in this decision. People's instinctive reaction may, however, be different.

Recent psychological studies on instinctive thinking of people suggest that *irrational* decisions may be made by people who are not trained to think in terms of the economic logic of the *sunk cost*, particularly when the problem is presented in a slightly more complicated way than in the above example. Let us consider the following example which is similar to the one cited by Daniel Kahneman who won Nobel Prize in economics in 2002 for his groundbreaking work in applying psychological insights into economic decision-making (Kahneman 2012, pp. 343–4). Suppose two friends residing in the same house are planning to go to watch a theatre show at a venue which is at quite a distance from their house. One of them has purchased his ticket, and the other was about to purchase a ticket when he got one free from a friend. On the evening of the show, heavy rains begin to pour in. Which of the two ticket holders is more likely to brave the rains to witness the show? The immediate answer is likely to be that the friend who paid for his ticket is more likely to go, but economic logic tells us that they both face the same choice. How?

A student of economics would realise that in making the decision the value of the ticket represents a *sunk* cost, whether the ticket is purchased or has been given as a gift. The decision to go or not should entirely depend on whether it is worth the trouble to go to the theatre hall to enjoy the show. If the friend who had purchased the ticket were himself an economics student, he would have been aware of the *counterfactual* possibility: Would I still go to the show if I had gotten the ticket free from a friend? It takes active and disciplined introspection to think in this way. Cool economic calculations do not acknowledge the emotions that people attach to their mental accounts.

Now, coming back to the earlier example of the development project which is already through one-third of its implementation, a parallel can be drawn by asking: Would it make a difference whether one should proceed towards completing the project if the cost already incurred was financed, alternatively, from the government's own budget or from a fund received freely as foreign assistance. The answer should be "no", assuming that the rest of the project cost would have to be borne by the government's own funds in either case. Apart from the psychological bias discussed above, another additional consideration may distort the decision-making in this case; the political cost for abandoning the project is likely to be more if the government is seen to have wasted domestic resources rather than free foreign assistance on an ill-planned project.

Saving difficulties of the poor

While economists themselves are trained to apply economic logic in their analysis of policy choice, they need also to take into account the fact that people do act differently from the *rational* individual described in the mainstream economic theory (the so-called "Econ" featured in the new field of behavioural economics). An example is provided by the saving behaviour of the poor. Economists have advanced various hypotheses to explain the saving difficulties of the poor in the developing countries, such as their livelihood risks that make it difficult for them to plan for the future, or an internalised psychology of fatalism, or their strong time preference that puts a very high premium on meeting immediate needs compared to the future needs.

Recent developments in behavioural economics have put forward another explanation for the saving difficulties of the poor, namely, the so-called *time-inconsistency* in intertemporal choice. The time-inconsistent behaviour of an individual refers to altered preferences between two points of time even if everything else were to remain the same and even without any benefit of hindsight and experience gathered between the two points of time (Thaler 2016, pp. 92–3, 99). This type of behaviour represents a kind of psychological barrier for implementing a plan; it may involve some kind of procrastination that separates the "doer" from the "planner" within oneself. The poor may thus need a so-called psychological "nudge" to help them implement their saving plan. For example, the microfinance institutions (MFIs) operating in various countries usually require their member-borrowers to keep compulsory savings, mainly as security against repayment default. But as the system gains maturity, as in Bangladesh which is regarded as the birthplace of microfinance, the members were induced by various means to voluntarily accumulate savings for use at times of need, and even to commit to long-term saving for old age. The various contractual saving schemes of the MFIs, like the Deposit Pension Scheme of Grameen Bank, were in fact designed to facilitate such a psychological commitment to long-run saving (Mahmud and Osmani 2017, pp. 220–3). The MFIs in Bangladesh were initially dependent mainly on foreign funds for their credit operations; by 2012, their member-borrowers' net savings had grown to about one-third of the total volume of their total revolving loan funds equivalent of more than US\$ 5 billion (Mahmud and Osmani 2017, pp. 17, 245).

While still on the topic of rational versus instinctive behaviour, we may recall a story caricaturing the folly of both people's instinctive behaviour and economists' overemphasis on making logical decisions.[7] An evolutionary biologist and an economist were taking a walk in a deep forest when they encountered a large bear aggressively confronting them. The biologist knew about the evolutionary human instinct of "fight or flee" and made the split-second decision to run. The economist sat down with his laptop to compute a model of optimal strategy. The biologist was killed by the bear because he was not aware of the advice given by every experienced forest ranger: stand still if you come face to face with a bear, never try to run away since it will catch up with you. The lesson: going by instinct does not always work, but there is also a right time and place for fine-tuning economic reasoning, since urgent situations may need urgent policy decisions. The economist in this story was lucky, but not for the right reason.

The Keynesian model and national income identities

The discussion on the concepts of national income in introductory textbooks is often followed by introducing the basic Keynesian model of macroeconomic equilibrium. Maynard Keynes, the most well-known economist of the twentieth century, used this model in the wake of the Great Depression of the 1930s in the Western industrialised economies to explain how unemployment for a prolonged period can occur in such economies due to lack of sufficient *aggregate demand* in the economy. The model, which laid the foundation of modern macroeconomics, can also serve as an illustration of how the same economic model can be viewed from very different perspectives in the context of industrialised vis-à-vis less developed countries. It also, incidentally, can be used to explain the difference between the so-called national income *identities* and the concept of an algebraic equation. National income or gross domestic product (GDP) is defined as the sum of the value of *final* goods and services produced during a given time, usually a year (we ignore here the other variants of national income such as gross national product [GNP] and gross national income [GNI]). The qualifying word *final* is important, since it avoids "double-counting", an important concept in national income accounting that guards against counting the value of an intermediate product or service, say, fertilisers used in rice production, since its value is already accounted for in valuing the final product, that is, rice. From the production side, GDP is thus estimated by adding what is called *value-added* across all production activities in the economy by netting out the total value of intermediate items from the *gross* value of output. While the concept of *value-added* has been made familiar in many developing countries by the introduction of the value-added tax (VAT), not many besides the students of economics are aware that GDP is the total value-added in an economy in a year, which, in turn, is also the total of all incomes generated in the economy in that year.

From the demand side, the output of any production activities can be used as intermediate items in another production activity or for *final* use for consumption (C) or investment (I) (to keep it simple, we assume a closed economy with no export and import). Non-economists do not often have a clear idea about investment, which in concrete terms means buying machinery or constructing factories, roads, etc., or investing in working capital in the form of adding to or depleting inventories of goods for business purposes. Thus, taking together all production activities, the use of (that is, expenditure on) total output for C and I can be obtained again by netting out the cost of intermediate items from the *gross* value of output. It follows, therefore, that in a closed economy, national income or GDP (Y) is *identically* equal to the sum of total consumption (C) and investment (I) in a year, that is, $Y = C + I$. Since the part of income (Y) which is not consumed is by definition saving (S), that is, $S = Y - C$, it also follows that total saving in the economy is also *identically* equal to total investment, that is, $I = S$. These are the so-called national income identities that always hold in a closed economy.

The above national income identities can lead to another puzzle for non-economists or for students studying introductory economics. Decisions for investments such as building a factory or buying production machinery are made by investors who are a relatively small proportion of the population, whereas those for saving are made by the large majority of households (and businesses) in the economy. Then how is it that the two on the aggregate have to be always equal in the annual national income accounts?

Total savings in the economy may in fact exceed the level of investment *intended* by investors, which will also mean that the total amount of goods and services that consumers and investors would like to buy will fall short of total goods and services that producers are willing to sell. The producers will thus be faced with an unintended build-up of inventories in excess of what is normally needed for maintaining smooth market supply. The level of production will thus tend to adjust downward causing economic contraction. This is the problem Keynes wanted to address through measures for boosting aggregate demand, such as by increasing government spending along with providing incentives for investors to invest more and for consumers to save less. In the Keynesian model, the macroeconomic equilibrium is established, and the national income *equations* hold, when aggregate demand is sufficiently high to match the full productive capacity of the economy (which Keynes called full employment in the context of industrialised countries).

However, what needs to be noted is that the national income *identities* will hold irrespective of whether the economy is at a full employment equilibrium or not. This is because of the way we define investment, so as to include both physical investment as well as investment in inventories. Even if aggregate demand falls short of full employment aggregate supply and there is excess build-up of inventories, the national income identities discussed above will still hold because investment, as defined above, will include all net additions to inventories, desired or not.

In contrast to the problem of deficient aggregate demand addressed in the Keynesian model, the labour-surplus developing countries chronically suffer from unemployment (in the form of underutilised labour in different forms) not so much because of lack of aggregate demand as of lack of enough production capacity. The production capacities in these economies are limited by low saving and investment rates along with a lack of technological development. In his pioneering paper, V. K. R. V. Rao elaborated this contrast between the industrialised and the less developed countries regarding the relevance of the Keynesian model (Rao 1952). Once the contrast is explained, one can proceed to show how the basic Keynesian model per se applies only obliquely to such an economy when suitably modified to explain such policy choices as increasing public investment through deficit financing.

The government may, for example, resort to investment by deficit financing to an extent that aggregate demand will tend to exceed aggregate supply, which also means that investment will tend to exceed saving, thus creating inflation and a consequent redistribution of income in the economy. This may increase aggregate savings by redistributing income in favour of the rich (profit-earners) who tend to save a relatively higher proportion of their income and away from the poor (wage labourers) who save at lower rates. The increased saving generated through inflation – known as "forced saving" – will thus match the higher investment. This way of generating saving will be, however, limited by the capacity of inflation to generate saving in this way and by the tolerable level of inflation – a phenomenon called the "inflationary barrier" to public investment. In the context of less developed economies, much of the discussions about the causes and consequences of inflation are discussed in this framework of excess demand, although there are also other approaches involving the monetary policy (the so-called "monetarist" theories of inflation). However, once we incorporate external trade in the Keynesian model, the national income identities and equations need to be adjusted for the external balance, and the macroeconomic policy options are also widened to include the impact of trade and exchange rate policies.

Analysing markets and institutions

Economics is mainly about analysing how markets work. The performance of an economy depends to a large extent on whether markets work badly or efficiently, and the functioning of markets, in turn, is determined not only by the quality of the regulatory framework under which they operate but also by the socio-cultural institutions in which they are embedded. To understand why some less developed countries perform better than others, it is thus important to analyse the functioning of markets in various formal and informal institutional settings that evolve over time. The variety of market institutions in less developed countries also makes it difficult to predict the outcomes of market intervention policies, such as the enforcement of an anti-monopoly regulation or the introduction of a value-added tax.

As noted earlier, economics students in developing countries have an advantage in this respect, if only they have an inquisitive mind. They have first-hand knowledge of observing the functioning of markets under very different institutional settings, representing various stages of development, varying from rural *hats* and *bazaars* to modern shopping malls in cities. Shabana Azmi, the noted Indian film actress and social activist, once remarked that India lived simultaneously in three centuries; that is certainly true of the varying nature of markets in less developed countries, such as in terms of the formal–informal divide, supply variability and price fluctuations in agricultural markets, product quality standards, integration with the global economy and so on. The students of economics can thus have an enriching experience in trying to apply the toolkits of market analysis across a variety of markets. Such analyses may vary in analytical sophistication, so as to suit the level of economics study – from the simple so-called cobweb model of annual agricultural price fluctuations to the testing of price expectation models in the context of food-grain market behaviour during food scarcities (Ravallion 1985), or the application of the theory of markets with imperfect information to explain why water-mixed adulterated milk pervades the *bazaars* in Dhaka (Rashid 1988).

Markets with information asymmetry

The 2001 Nobel Prize in economics went to George Akerlof, Joseph Stiglitz and Michael Spence, whose contributions laid the foundation of what is now known as the theory of markets with imperfect information. The theory breaks away from the traditional neoclassical economics by introducing market situations characterised by asymmetric information between actors on two sides of the market: borrowers know more than lenders about their loan repayment prospects, sellers are often a better judge of the quality of their products than are buyers and prospective employees know more about their abilities than does the employer. In their theorising, both Akerlof and Stiglitz had in mind mainly markets in a developing country setting.

Akerlof's theory, for example, can be applied in a simple way to explain why in the Delhi open market most of the milk available used to be once adulterated by mixing water with pure milk.[8] How did this happen? Suppose, to start with, there was only a small proportion of adulterated milk in the market. Since the buyers could not distinguish between the watered and the pure milk, they would be ready to buy at a price which would reflect the small probability of getting the adulterated milk. That price would be a good incentive for the dishonest seller, but less so for the honest ones. So more dishonest sellers will enter the market and the honest sellers will be discouraged. Buyers will then know by experience that the probability of getting adulterated milk has become higher, so they will offer even less price, which in turn will bring in more dishonest sellers and further drive out the honest ones. The process will continue until only adulterated milk is available in the market. The situation began to improve in the Delhi market when the authorities started a campaign for improving the quality of milk by introducing inexpensive devices to examine the water and butterfat contents of milk at different points of the supply chain.

Akerlof had to find a market familiar to his fellow Americans, so he theorised the problem of market with imperfect information in his 1970 seminal paper, "The Market for Lemons", by using the example of the second-hand car market ("lemons" is a colloquialism for defective old cars and resembles the informational characteristics of watered milk in the Delhi market). But he intended the paper to give a theoretical structure to explain why "business in underdeveloped countries is difficult". In affluent countries, this informational problem is solved by various means of quality assurance, such as product standardisation, labelling and packaging and promotion of product branding for reputation. But this remains a serious problem in many less developed countries resulting in markets functioning poorly. In the absence of strong market regulatory measures and product standardisation, markets are often pervaded by inferior or even harmful products ranging from adulterated food items to low-quality medicines, thus posing a serious threat to public health as well as resulting in various kinds of "transaction costs" for buyers in identifying good-quality products.

Stiglitz was considering rural credit markets in less developed countries. In particular, he analysed the problem of providing a collateral-free business loan to a poor prospective micro-entrepreneur. Since the lender has no means to monitor how the loan is actually used and can recover the loan only if the business venture is successful (implying "limited liability" for the borrower), the risk of the business failure is borne entirely by the lender. The borrower may thus go for more profitable but riskier projects and also spend less effort on the project, compared to what the lender would like her to do; the result is an inefficient credit market. In the theoretical literature on microfinance, this problem is called ex ante moral hazard as distinct from ex post moral hazard; the latter has to do with the recovery of the loan after the loan has been used, successfully or not.[9] Stiglitz further theorised how the introduction of the Grameen Bank's microcredit programme in Bangladesh sought to solve this problem of ex ante moral hazard through a system of group lending; the members of the group monitored one another's use of loan because of the joint-liability for loan repayment, thus removing the problem of moral hazard.[10]

Ironically, however, the above logic of moral hazard may be less true for a mature microfinance system than for the formal banking system in many less developed countries with poor enforcement of loan recovery. The logic does not apply if the foreseen cost of non-repayment in the mental calculation of the borrower at the time of using the loan is high enough to ensure that she (he) is not contemplating non-repayment regardless of the success or failure of the project for which the loan is taken. Mahmud and Osmani (2017, pp. 44–8, 53–5) found that this was indeed so in the case of microfinance in Bangladesh; the well-established practice of loan repayment had become part of a social norm in a way so that the borrowers felt like bearing the "full liability" of repayment rather than the "limited liability" related to the success or failure of the project, as assumed in Stiglitz's model. The mental calculation of cost of non-repayment on the part of the borrowers has much to do with the social stigma attached to being branded as a defaulter and breaching of a trust-based relationship with the lender (e.g., the microfinance institutions), along with the material cost of being deprived of further loans. This provides an example of how economic theorising may fail to keep pace with the field-level new realities.

Agricultural markets

The markets for agricultural products in less developed countries are often characterised by large price fluctuations, which are often explained in the introductory texts on agricultural economics in terms of the so-called cobweb model. The model deviates from the usual supply–demand market model by assuming that the supply (production) of a crop responds to the market price only with a time lag; the supply this year is determined by the price prevalent in the previous year, while this year's price will determine farmer's decision of production next year, and so on. This may lead to considerable annual price fluctuations, adversely affecting farmers' production incentives. While the model can provide useful insights, actual market outcomes for agricultural products may be quite different, depending on how both supply and demand are affected by a host of other non-price factors, such as government market interventions or the impact of any international trade in those products.

In the 1990s, when I was doing a study along with some researchers from the Bangladesh Institute of Development Studies on the relative profitability of crops in Bangladesh, we gained some fresh perspectives on the cobweb model (Mahmud et al. 2000). As expected, the variations in the production and price of rice, the staple food crop, have very little to do with the cobweb model. Leaving aside the long-run trend in the growth of rice production due to the adoption of high-yielding technologies, there is not much scope for farmers' response to price fluctuations since rice cultivation already accounts for much of the cropped land in a year. While annual rice harvests may be affected to an extent by the vagaries of nature, the potential price shocks are muted by the government's regular market interventions through the system of public food grain procurement and distribution.

The case of some minor crops is, however, a different story with a very high annual price variability. We found that, for the preceding decade, the *average* annual price deviations (positive and negative signs ignored) around the estimated *trend* level (a kind of annual projected price for the period under review) varied between 15 to 25 percent for fruits and vegetables and 20 to 40 percent for spices. This means that the year-to-year price fluctuations, say, from above the trend price in one year to below the trend in the next year were way much higher than what were suggested by these estimates of average deviations. These are mostly high-value crops and much more profitable compared to rice, but because of the very high price risks, farmers usually grow one or more of these crops on small plots and also rotate the crops from year to year. The supply can thus vary to a very large extent depending on farmers' price expectations. Although the extent of price variability for some of these crops was found to be too high to allow any rational price expectation, one can reasonably assume a kind of cobweb model to play a role in this case. As we could see, the way to address the problem was by country-wide dissemination of real-time information among farmers regarding the arable area being devoted to a particular crop, which was not easy at that time. But, with the currently widespread internet access through mobile phones, the government's agricultural extension agencies are now moving towards gathering such real-time information on cropping patterns.

There are many other ways in which agricultural markets in less developed countries work poorly. For example, it is a common practice in South Asia to use harmful chemicals (mostly, calcium carbide) to ripen fruits like mangoes, bananas, litchis and jackfruits. These chemicals are highly hazardous to human health and there are laws prohibiting their use, but these laws are only poorly implemented, if at all. Traders pick fruits before maturation to take advantage of the early-season high prices and also because of the ease of transportation of green fruits with minimum damage and ripening them artificially at the points of retail sale. But there is more to it. The farmers have to weigh the increasing risk of theft of the fruits during the ripening time against the lower prices they get for harvesting the fruits before the proper time. This again adds to the reason why the fruits need to be ripened artificially. While all the actors involved are looking after their self-interest, the extent to which the "invisible hand" of the market system results in public welfare thus depends on the socio-cultural settings into which the system is embedded.

In the markets for food items in less developed countries, there are often price hikes during certain festival seasons; for example, certain food items are especially in high demand in the Muslim majority countries during the fasting month of Ramadan. It is possible that market manipulations by trade syndicates may be partly to blame, but in most cases the phenomenon can be explained by supply lagging behind demand, given the perishable nature of the food items or their high storage costs or, in the case of imported items, the uncertainty in global supply and prices. While traders are usually blamed by the media and the politicians for their *unethical* act of taking advantage of the market situation at a time of religious festivity, it does not occur to many that the moral responsibility must also then be borne in part by the relatively wealthy buyers who may choose to apply some moderation in consuming the items in demand, so that the prices rise less steeply and the limited supply is more equitably shared by all. An *ethical* comparison is also made sometimes by contrasting such price hikes with the so-called Christmas sales in the West. In fact, there is nothing ethical about those year-end Christmas sales, mostly consisting of clothing items. The store managers observe during the pre-Christmas shopping season which items are not in demand anymore, so that it makes perfect economic sense to put those items on sale instead of wasting storage space on them.

Overcrowding of micro-enterprises and scaling up

One important characteristic of less developed countries, as pointed out by Abhijit Banerjee and Esther Duflo (2011, pp. 215–8), is the proliferation of small businesses like roadside shops, vending, hawking and petty trading; this represents a wastage of manpower and lack of opportunities for growth through scaling up of enterprises. They also point out that the inability of the self-employed poor to scale up their businesses beyond subsistence results in their having multiple occupations, which prevents them from acquiring skills and experience in their main occupation. Mahmud and Osmani (2017, pp. 225–30) looked at the evidence regarding the problems faced by the clients of the Microfinance Institutions (MFIs) in Bangladesh in scaling up their business enterprises by borrowing larger amounts of loans that the MFIs were willing to offer. While the returns to investment are quite high in subsistence-type businesses, the potential tapers off quite fast with the increase in the size of the enterprise. The returns are high to start with due to some advantages derived from the subsistence-type characteristics of these enterprises, such as the availability of unpaid family help, free use of homestead space or common property resources and personalised nature of marketing of products. These advantages start to disappear quickly as soon as there is an attempt to expand the enterprise size bit by bit; instead, it requires a jump to a much higher level of investment to shift to produc-tion and marketing technologies that are economically viable at a higher scale of operation. An evidence of this, for example, is provided by the fact that the few relatively successful members of the mainstream microcredit programmes seek significantly larger loans, not just incrementally larger loans, if they want to expand their businesses, and also that the majority of the MFI clients who take larger-sized loans are lateral entrants rather than graduates of the mainstream programmes.

According to Mahmud and Osmani (2017, pp. 227–8), the explanation of this phenomenon may lie at least partly in a "technology gap" or a "miss-ing middle" that prevents a process of gradual scaling up through any incre-mental change in the size of businesses, but requires a quantum shift in scale and technology. The challenge for the MFIs and their "entrepreneur-ial" clients is to find ways of bridging this "technology gap" in innovative ways by supporting and adopting appropriate production and marketing

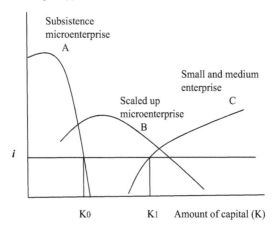

Figure 2.2 Scaling up of micro-enterprises by bridging the technology gap.

strategies (Figure 2.2). The PKSF, which is an apex institution for whole-sale funding of the microfinance programmes in Bangladesh (and of which the present author is a founder and a former chairman), has been providing support to its partner MFIs towards this end with some success. Banerjee and Duflo (2011, p. 222), in a similar context, show diagrammatically how a transition can be made from a subsistence technology to a superior one, but without recognising the possibility of any such technology gap.

In Figure 2.2, the amount of capital invested (K), including both fixed and working capital, is measured along X-axis and the *marginal* rate of return to capital r along Y-axis; the return is profit net of wage cost, including the imputed cost of the unpaid family worker. Assume that loans are available at the interest rate i. The curve A represents the technology of a typical subsistence-type enterprise of microcredit borrowers. Although it provides very high returns to capital to start with, the marginal rate of return declines quickly to equal the interest rate (e.g., $i = r$) at the amount of capital K0, beyond which point it becomes therefore unprofitable to expand the enterprise. The curve C, on the other hand, represents a superior technology of small and medium enterprises that needs some minimum amount of capital investment before it reaches its potential and becomes profitable at the point K1 and beyond. With these two technologies, it therefore requires a discrete jump in capital investment from K0 to K1 to increase the size of the enterprise. It can be seen, however, that as soon as we introduce an innovative "bridging" technology represented by B, it becomes possible to make a smooth incremental transition by scaling up the micro-enterprises beyond subsistence, eventually to small and medium enterprises, while remaining profitable at the given interest rate. (Notice that in this diagrammatic exposition we need not explicitly show labour use, but can assume that technology C will be relatively more capital intensive compared to technology A.)

In the field of poverty and market interventions in the less developed countries, there may be many such observed phenomena that can be better understood by applying economic logic. Development practitioners at the field level often apply a learning-by-doing approach to know what interventions work and what do not. They also have ideas and insights from experience that are often missed by academic experts. Economists, on the other hand, have the toolkits to formalise the ideas of practitioners into theories and put them to rigorous empirical tests. This, in turn, can help further policy innovations, thus enriching both theorising and practice of development interventions.

Notes

1 Quoted in Mankiw (2004), p. 32.
2 See, for example, Bardhan and Udry (1999); Basu, Kaushik (1997) and Ray, Debraj (1998).
3 Foreword by Vargas Llosa, in de Soto (1989, p. xi). He made this comment in relation to the story of how Peru's poor make a living through black markets in Lima.
4 See, for example, Frey and Meier (2005).
5 Cf. His interview with the *Brain World* magazine (New York, June 8, 2019).
6 The friend being mentioned here is Syed M. Ahsan, Professor Emeritus of Economics at Concordia University, Canada.
7 For another version of the story of an economist confronting a bear, see Kay (2004), p. 219.
8 See, for example, McMillan (2002), p. 51.
9 For numerical examples on this, see Ray (1998), pp. 532–4.
10 For detailed discussions on the nature of rural credit markets and the effectiveness of the microcredit system, see, for example, Mahmud and Osmani (2017), Chapters 2 and 3.

References

Banerjee, A. and Duflo, E. (2011). *Poor Economics: A Radical Rethinking of the Way to Fight Global Poverty*. New York: Public Affairs.

Bardhan, P. and Udry, C. (1999). *Development Microeconomics*. Oxford: Oxford University Press.

Basu, Kaushik. (1997). *Analytical Development Economics: The Less Developed Economy Revisited*. Cambridge, MA: The MIT Press.

de Soto, Hernando. (1989). *The Other Path*. New York: Harper and Row.

Frey, Bruno and Meier, Stephen. (2005). "Selfish and indoctrinated economists?". *European Journal of Law and Economics*, Vol. 19, pp. 165–71.

Kahneman, D. (2012). *Thinking Fast and Slow*. UK: Penguin Random House.

Kay, J. (2004). *Culture and Prosperity: Why Some Nations Are Rich but Most Remain Poor*. New York: HarperCollins.

Keynes, J. Maynard. (1972). *Essays in Biography*. London: Macmillan/St. Martin's Press for the Royal Economic Society.

McMillan, John. (2002). *Reinventing the Bazaar, A Natural History of Markets*. New York: W. W. Norton & Company.

Mahmud, W. (1989). "The impact of overseas migration on the Bangladesh economy: A macroeconomic perspective". In R. Amjad (ed.), *To the Gulf and Back*. New Delhi: UNDP and ILO.

Mahmud, W. (2014). "Mozena versus Tofail: Who pays for US tariff on Bangladesh's garment export?", *The Daily Star*, Dhaka, Nov. 16.

Mahmud, W. and Osmani, Siddiq. (2017). *The Theory and Practice of Microcredit*. Abingdon, UK: Routledge.

Mahmud, W., Rahman, S. H. and Zohir, S. (2000). "Agricultural growth through crop diversification in Bangladesh". In R. Ahmed, S. Haggblade, S. and T. Chowdhury (eds.), *Out of the Shadow of Famine: Evolving Food Markets and Food Policy in Bangladesh*, Chapter 12, pp. 236–237. Baltimore and London: The Johns Hopkins University Press.

Mankiw, W. G. (2004). *Principles of Economics*, 3rd edition. Mason, OH: South Western Mason.

Pigou, A. C. (ed.). (1925). *Memorials of Alfred Marshall*. London: Macmillan

Rao, V. K. R. V. (1952). "Investment, income, and the multiplier in an underdeveloped economy". *Indian Economic Review*, Vol. 1, pp. 55–67.

Rashid, Salim. (1988). "The quality in contestable markets: A historical problem". *Quarterly Journal of Economics*, Vol. 98 (March), pp. 245–249.

Ravallion, M. (1985). "The performance of rice market during the 1974 famine". *Economic Journal*, Vol. 95 (March).

Ray, Debraj. (1998). *Development Economics*. NJ, USA: Princeton University Press.

Samuelson, Paul A. (1969). "The way of an economist". In P. A. Samuelson (ed.), *International Economic Relations*: *Proceedings of the Third Congress of the International Economic Association*, pp. 1–11. London: Macmillan.

Thaler, Richard H. (2016). *Misbehaving: The Making of Behavioural Economics*. UK: Penguin Random House.

Tirole, J. (2007). *Economics for the Common Good*. Princeton, NJ: Princeton University Press.

3 The ethical basis of economic theory and practice

Moral philosophy is not regarded as a strong point of academic economists. Oscar Wilde defined a cynic as someone who knows the price of everything and the value of nothing, and it is widely believed that he was pointing towards economists. Carlyle held a similarly dim view of economics as a discipline when he termed it as a dismal science. Economists, in turn, feel wrongly accused, for they are usually not the cause of dismal happenings but simply the messengers. The strongest link between economics and the real world has always been politics, which is why economics used to be called "political economy", for it is the politicians who make the choice about how to put economics into practice. Economists also cannot help if people in their economic dealings act selfishly; as Adam Smith, in one of his famous statements, warned that businessmen seldom meet without plotting against the consumer. The purpose of this chapter is to review and rethink the state of economics as a discipline in light of how and to what extent ethical considerations and the precepts of moral philosophy affect the theory and application of economics.[1]

Can profit motive alone explain the working of markets?

The entire body of the theory of price and market is based on the assumption that markets function on the basis of producers and suppliers trying to maximise their profits while buyers or consumers try to maximise their satisfaction. The key role of the profit motive in economic theorising goes back to Adam Smith who was a believer in the virtues of the so-called "invisible hand" guiding the market through the self-interested behaviour of businessmen. As he made it clear: "it is not from the benevolence of the butcher … or the baker that we expect our dinner, but from their regard to their own interest". In other words, both buyers and sellers (producers), acting out of their self-interest, can benefit from market transactions. This

DOI: 10.4324/9781003241775-3

was the origin of how *rational* behaviour in economics defined in terms of self-interest was implicitly given a moral validity.

While the ethical issue regarding self-interested behaviour, or the universal validity of this assumption in real-life economic behaviour, may be subject to debate, its role in the functioning of the market remains generally valid. Markets embody a vast amount of information, without which efforts for doing good to others may sometimes lead to unforeseen consequences. One has to only recollect O Henry's story "The Gift of the Magi" to see how the uninformed pursuit of love and altruism can lead to frustration. If businessmen in their economic decision-making were to be guided by philanthropy rather than profit motive, the market could hardly function in any coherent manner. A market-equilibrium price cannot be reached if both the seller and the buyer want to do good to each other instead of acting out of self-interest. It is not uncommon for a housewife from a well-off family to engage in hard bargaining with a poor *ferrywallah* (street vendor), settle a price and then give him some extra money out of compassion. In our day-to-day dealings, we thus show different personality traits; we are part "human" but also part "econ" – the self-seeking individual as portrayed in the economics textbook.[2] Modern psychological research also suggests that making a choice related to money encourages in people a "business-like mindset" that is less trusting and generous. Incidentally, the term "econ" has been used in the recent literature on behavioural economics; more traditional literature used the term *homo economicus*.

Two questions arise: first, can the profit motive alone explain the working of markets? While human behaviour is complex with various traits, the question is about the extent to which the self-seeking trait can be isolated from others to explain the functioning of market, the mainstay of economic theory. The common acts of philanthropy, of course, affect income distribution along with other macroeconomic outcomes, but we are primarily concerned here with the neoclassical theory of market and price. Second, are all self-seeking market transactions necessarily welfare-enhancing, as claimed by many to be implicit in Smith's advocacy of the invisible hand of the market? If not, does one need to interpret the welfare implications of market transactions depending on the contexts in which such transactions take place?

Beyond profit motive

It is not difficult to find certain markets which cannot be explained by the self-seeking motive alone. Nobel laureate (2014) economist Jean Tirole gives the example in which paying for blood donation, or increasing the amount of such payment, does not necessarily increase the amount of blood given (Tirole 2016). People may be worried that if they are paid more, or paid at all, their contribution will feel like (or will be interpreted by others as) greed rather than generosity. Higher financial rewards in this market may not thus increase the supply of blood.

Beyond some such specific instances, there are broader ethical considerations that are increasingly drawing public attention to market outcomes, particularly as frustration grows about some adverse consequences of modern-day global capitalism. There are, for example, consumer campaigns aimed at increasing awareness about the ethical standards of business practices regarding the supply chains of production and the sourcing of raw materials. Examples include the alleged destruction of forests by indiscriminate logging to supply wood to the large furniture companies, or the environmental and health risks arising from diamond and gold mining, or the lack of labour standards in factories in developing countries producing consumer items for the rich countries. However, while representing genuine consumer concerns, some of these campaigns may also be driven in part by the protectionist lobbies in the industrialised countries, such as in the case of ready-made garment export from countries like Bangladesh.

In response to changes in consumer attitudes, companies worldwide are increasingly incorporating in their business model some strategic elements of corporate social responsibility (CSR) that can be in their long-run business interest. Such an approach to CSR, which is different from traditional corporate philanthropy of setting aside some profits for social spending, can be seen as a way of delivering some social good, such as promoting healthy foods or cleaner fuels or low-priced generic drugs, with the long-run objective of cashing on the goodwill thus created for the company. There is an increasing interest in the global business community in what is called "impact investments", that is, investments made by companies and other organisations with the intention to generate social and environmental impact alongside a financial return. This represents a departure, albeit in a limited sense, from the often-quoted statement allegedly made by Milton Friedman: "the business of business is business", implying that the sole legitimate purpose of business is to maximise profit.

Successful entrepreneurs also know that good businesses have to be built on public trust. The now-defunct oil giant, Enron, turned from one of the best-rated companies in the United States into perhaps the most hated one when it was revealed that nobody outside its boardroom quite understood what it was doing other than engaging in huge financial frauds. American public opinion about tobacco companies became sour not because of their marketing a harmful product, but when company documents were leaked to show that they had long pretended not to know about the mounting evidence of the hazards of smoking. The gruesome corporate shenanigans led

John le Carre to write his sensational novel *The Constant Gardener*; in an interview about the book he strongly refuted the view held by many that "at the centre of corporations lies a moral purpose, some humanitarian self-restraint" (McMillan 2002). It cannot be assumed that people or corporations will behave well. The challenge of market design is to devise mechanisms, including the formal device of law and the informal device of reputation and trust that channel the pursuit of profits in a socially productive direction.

Beyond such instances of outright dishonesty, there are also more subtle aspects of corporate ethics (e.g., employee welfare or fairness in recruitment policies) that may not be cost-effective for businesses but positively affect public sensibilities. Business management is also influenced by cultural factors like the structures of cooperation or feelings of solidarity which do not always represent the individualist self-seeking behaviour. For example, it was once argued by some economists that the so-called "Japanese ethos" of loyalty of the Japanese workers to their firm and to their co-workers rather than individual self-seeking was the key to the success of the Japanese economy (Morishima 1982).

The motivation behind entrepreneurship at the individual level is another behavioural aspect that does not fit easily with theory, since it may be a kind of satisfaction other than what is derived from earning money for material pleasure (i.e., textbook utility maximisation). How would one, for example, explain the fact that Warren Buffet, known to be one of the world's richest men, lives modestly in a "Omaha bungalow and enjoys nothing more than a Nebraska steak washed down with Cherry Coke". As he remarked in his autobiographical book: "It is the fun of making money and watching it grow" (Lowenstein 1995). Keynes attempted an explanation in terms of what he called "animal spirits", an urge for action to build up a business; animal spirits for him were neither rational nor irrational.

The desire for material satisfaction or the "animal spirits" of the entrepreneurs need to be distinguished from obsessive greed, since the latter has moral undertones and may lead to undesirable economic consequences and human miseries. The self-destructive nature of greed is amply portrayed in such literary works as Leo Tolstoy's story, "How Much Land Does a Man Need" or American playwright Arthur Miller's *Death of a Salesman*. The repeated episodes of bursts and bubbles in the financial markets such as the recent ones in the United States, which are attributed largely to the irrational greed of the actors in those markets, defy explanation by the economic theories of financial markets. Even though Robert Merton and Myron Scholes were awarded Nobel Prize in 1997 and Robert Shiller in 2013 for their contributions in this field, a better understanding of the causes of financial crises may need an interdisciplinary approach by drawing from the recent studies on neuroscience and experimental psychology that investigate the role of expectation of financial gains, and addiction and risk-taking in making choices. For example, according to Professor Colin F. Camerer, a proponent of "neuroeconomics" at the California Institute of Technology, the role of emotional (or, irrational) actions is likely to be a key factor behind the episodes of financial crises. Regarding the financial crisis of 2008, Camerer would like to view it through the lens of a typical "Agatha Christie novel in which everyone is guilty ... emotions, greed, blind extrapolation of housing prices, and opaque institutions with slippages in regulation all played a part".[3]

Are all market transactions welfare-enhancing or fair?

The implication of the Smithian analysis of the "invisible hand" that self-interested free market exchanges are beneficial for all market participants is explained further by the neoclassical theory of consumers' and producers' surplus. While admitting the logic of this argument, economic textbooks discuss various market imperfections that call for policy interventions to improve the welfare-enhancing role of the market. The most notable example is how promoting free competition to break up market monopolies can increase welfare (illustrated by the familiar diagram of how monopolies, compared to perfect competition, create "deadweight loss" in terms of the net effect on consumers' and producers' surplus).

There are various other kinds of market imperfections that make the welfare-enhancing role of free market transactions doubtful. For example, an individual firm's production can harm others by, say, creating pollution – the so-called negative production externalities – which again call for policy interventions, such as imposing an appropriate tax to account for the social cost of such pollution. Again, a market exchange may be unacceptable when a third-party interest is adversely affected; there may be thus a legitimate case for legislating against child labour, particularly when the work involved can be hazardous to health (children being the third party in this case). The moral limits to markets are also exemplified by, say, the ban on trade in human organs or slave trade or certain forms of prostitution. Imperfect information about product quality can also lead to sub-standard or even harmful products, as analysed by Nobel laureate (2001) economist George Akerlof in his seminal essay, "The Markets for Lemons" (Akerlof 1970). The issue is not whether there should be regulation in such cases to protect public interest, but the nature and extent of such regulation, which is a matter of social values, judgement and empirical evidence.

On the consumers' side, there is the obvious case for banning or regulating markets for addictive drugs on the ground of adverse social effects (i.e., the consumption externalities) and also because, in society's judgement, an individual may not be the best judge of his own welfare in certain circumstances. The later ground, however, raises ethical questions regarding where to draw the borderline in restricting individual preference.

There are also other less-discussed issues about consumption externalities that are related to the societal value system. People often tend to use the material possessions of their neighbours as a benchmark for judging their own living standards, as reflected in the well-known idiom of "keeping up with the Joneses". This has implications for the psychological well-being of the disadvantaged in an unequal society. Even broader ethical questions are raised about the materialism and consumerism of the currently developed countries being taken as an "aspiration model" for imitation by less developed countries, particularly in an age of globalisation. As argued by environmentalists, the adoption of such consumerism globally, driven by modern-day capitalism, may become unsustainable given the limits to the earth's natural resources. Even though the analysis of social constructs of consumerism is beyond the scope of mainstream economics, a rethinking of the ideas of human well-being and incorporating those in economic analyses can be a way for economists to contribute to this vitally important issue.

Unequal power and fairness

A deeper moral issue arises concerning market transactions between parties with unequal economic power that may be regarded as "exploitative". If a beggar agrees to work 16 hours a day in exchange for a bare minimum subsistence of food and shelter, the arrangement can be viewed as *unfair*, even though both parties may be rational, well-informed and both may enter the arrangement willingly. The exploitative nature of traditional money-lending in poor communities is well-known, and governments often made legislations to put a limit to the exorbitant interest rate charged, though often without success. As Nobel laureate (1972) economist John Hicks remarks in his book titled *The Theory of Economic History*: "Lawmakers and judges at all ages were tormented on the issue of recovery of unsecured loans that represent contracts freely arrived at and yet cannot be enforced without 'oppression'" (Hicks 1969, pp. 76–7). There is an entire literature, mostly in the context of rural India, about how the semi-feudal relationship between a landlord and his tenants can become even more exploitative when the landlord is also the lender and the employer of his tenant (Bardhan and Udry 1999, pp. 110–12). While given his poverty, the tenant enters these contracts willingly, the policy interventions should focus on remedying his situation by changing the power structure, say, by introducing land reforms, ensuring tenancy rights, providing easy excess to the formal credit market or by even broader policies of poverty alleviation.

Much of the debates on globalisation can also be seen in the above alternative perspectives on the welfare implications of free market transactions, namely (a) within the narrow confines of neoclassical theory of, say, trade liberalisation benefiting both rich and poor countries, or (b) in terms of the *fairness* in the distribution of gains from the arrangements, given the asymmetry of global power structure with the poverty of the poor countries and opulence of the rich countries. Jagdish Bhagwati's book titled *In Defence of Globalization* (Bhagwati 2004) represents the former viewpoint, while Joseph Stiglitz's *Globalization and Its Discontents* (Stiglitz 2002) reflects the later viewpoint. The proponents of globalisation typically argue, and rightly so in most cases, that the poor countries would be poorer without freer trade. The critiques, on the other hand, point out the various biases in the global arrangements, such as under the World Trade Organization (WTO), in favour of the richer and more powerful countries. The biases are reflected, for example, in the way patent rights are enforced or in selective liberalisation of global markets in which exports from the industrialised countries have more to gain, while keeping restrictions on items of interest for the less developed countries.

Rudiger Dornbush, the late MIT economist, once remarked that it is a reasonable guess that to a Martian visitor observing our planet's economy, the most striking puzzle would be as to why a worker in a less developed country makes a tiny fraction of the wage of a worker in the United States doing a similar manual job. A possible answer to this query is to tell the Martian that he is being naïve and that he should go back to where he came from. But alternative answers could express concern not only about restrictions on the flow of unskilled labour across borders (while those of capital and high-skilled manpower are mostly encouraged), but also about the trade barriers that are sought against products that use low-wage labour in poor countries. It can be argued that if freer trade can be mutually beneficial for both poor and rich countries, it is up to domestic policymakers to see that those benefits are fairly distributed *within* the countries. As Nobel laureate (2008) economist Paul Krugman commented in an article in *The New York Times* (February 13, 1997): "None of the important constraints on American economic and social policy come from abroad". He argues that the US economy has enough resources to take far better care of the poor and the unlucky than is currently done, and that if the policies in this respect have increasingly become "mean-spirited", that is a political choice. He thus concludes: "We cannot evade responsibility for our actions by claiming that the global markets made us to do it".[4]

Lawrence Summers, while he was the Chief Economist at the World Bank in the early 1990s, wrote a memorandum to some colleagues making a *logical* case for the dumping of developed countries' toxic waste in poor countries. He argued that the cost of health-impairing pollution depends on the foregone earnings from increased morbidity and mortality and hence there is an "impeccable" case for dumping toxic waste in the lowest-wage countries, presumably with some compensation to make it a win–win deal. On the same ground, he further made a case for the relocation of polluting industries to poorer countries, given the high transportation costs of solid waste. Further, since the demand for a cleaner environment for aesthetic and health reasons is higher in rich countries than in poorer countries with lower income and longevity, trade in goods that embody such pollution could be welfare-enhancing. While Summers' economic logic is exemplary, he made the mistake of putting into words uncomfortable implications that most economists would prefer not to draw in a memo that might be leaked to *The Economist* (February 8, 1992, p. 66; Hausman and McPherson 1996, p. 10).

Hidden behind the above logic, there are several ethical considerations. Measuring the economic value of life by earnings foregone is ethically distasteful in any case, but may be unavoidable in certain circumstances, such as in deciding about compensation for deaths caused by, say, a factory accident. But considering life to be of less worth in a poorer country than in a richer country is an altogether different proposition and will be morally unacceptable to many. If it is a question of two parties entering willingly into a mutually beneficial arrangement, then it raises the question of "exploitation" through unequal economic power, as discussed earlier. Moreover, since the quality of environment is a "public good" not amenable to private market transactions, it is up to the respective governments to decide how they value the health-related well-being of their citizens. One can also ask the question: Even if such a trade in polluting goods or relocation of polluting industries may be mutually beneficial, given the poverty of the less developed countries, why should the World Bank spend efforts and resources to support such a seemingly unethical proposition? Instead, why not focus on poverty alleviation in those less developed countries, which would contribute to ultimately weaken the logic of such a proposition? Clearly, an apparently neat economic logic can become very complex once the ethical considerations are brought to bear on it.[5]

The limits of welfare economics

Welfare without value judgement?

It may appear paradoxical that the branch of neoclassical economics that is designated as "welfare economics" is akin to the core theory of the discipline in being devoid of making any value judgement, such as about fairness and justice. This is not only because of the premise of materialistic self-interest underlying the neoclassical theory, of which welfare economics is an integral part, but also because of the self-imposed limitation of the discipline in sticking to only "objective" analyses. As a result, there is no scope for accommodating even such a common-sense view of fairness that the value of an extra dollar is worth more to a beggar than to Bill Gates; it is sufficient for the theory to only assume, without going into "subjective" inter-personal comparison of well-being, that the value of additional dollars continuously declines for each individual separately. Nobel (1998) laureate economist Amartya Sen, for example, has often lamented about both these limitations of the economic theory, namely, the single-minded emphasis on the profit motive and what he calls the "informational crisis" of the theory in making any value judgement. Fortunately, he says, the real world is richer in human qualities than described in economics textbook (Sen 1984).

That the theoretical constructs of economics, being value-free and detached from social contexts, may appear to be far removed from one's perception of the real world is amply illustrated by an incident described by Tirole (2016, pp. 155–6). In December 1999, Jean-Jacques Laffont, the best-known French economist of his generation, presented his report to the Council of Economic Analysis (an advisory body appointed by the then Prime Minister of France) regarding the pathway for France to a modern state. The report, which was well articulated in economic terms, was greeted with an outcry by the audience of senior officials and bureaucrats, implying that he had understood nothing about the French society and politics. As one panellist remarked: "I don't want to live in the world you describe".

The traditional view of welfare dating back to the work of Jeremy Bentham in the late eighteenth century used to be the simple utilitarian one, judging social welfare by the sum of individual utilities, that is, the satisfaction derived from material acquisition (call it, say, "utils" for the purpose of measurement). Neoclassical economics, in its pursuit to be "objective" and attain the status of science, has rendered the utilitarian approach, along with many other related procedures, unworkable. As a result, welfare economics is severely constrained in making social judgements, particularly in matters of fairness and justice in which individual preferences conflict.

The so-called "fundamental theorems of welfare economics" as derived from the neoclassical theoretical constructs are limited to the concepts of "efficiency", alternatively called Pareto optimality, that obtains in a world of perfectly competitive market economy. The perfectly competitive market itself is an ideal situation that is never actually realised, so that it is taken only as a point of departure in order to introduce various market imperfections or market failures, which then warrant policy interventions. Pareto optimality describes a situation in which the well-being of no individual (defined in terms of satisfaction from material possession) can be increased without reducing that of another; hence there will exist scope for improvement of well-being for at least some in the society if a situation is not Pareto optimal. But there is nothing in this welfare criteria to make a judgement when there is a trade-off between the well-being of one individual with that of another; this is a severe limitation of theory for devising policies to improve the outcomes of a market economy, since most such policies involve some conflict of interest. There is a further concept of "compensation principle" involving Pareto optimality which is satisfied if the gains of an individual are large enough to potentially compensate the loss of another, but this begs the question of whether it is practically possible to redistribute the gains in this way. No wonder the contemporary "Paretian" welfare economics is considered to be of surprisingly limited help in evaluating economic institutions and outcomes.

One may argue that the narrow definitions of rationality or optimality have helped construct an elegant theory of the competitive market, which can be taken only as a point of departure. But that may be said as well about other approaches to theorising, such as defining satisfaction to include some element of empathy along with self-interest. According to a long-forgotten strand of economic theorising, the success of a competitive free-enterprise economy can be shown to depend on people pursuing *self-chosen* interest, which can be altruistic or anything else (Winter 1969). Similarly, Hirsch (1977) shows how behavioural modification, by breaking away from individual self-interest in certain situations, such as the "Japanese ethos" model of the firm mentioned earlier, can help better achieve the fulfilment of those very interests. Paul Samuelson, the *guru* of modern economic theory, devised a highly abstract multi-period model of overlapping generations, in which the working-age population save to pay for providing social security to the elderly in the expectation that the next generation will do so for them; in this model, a perfectly competitive market driven by self-interest may not result in the optimal outcome unless there is an ethical element of trust in the form of, say, a social contract (Samuelson 1958). However, it remains true that as long as individuals put their own interests above those of others, adding a dose of empathy to *homo economicus* will not much improve the market paradigm's power to explain how individuals actually behave in their economic dealings.

What about extending the concept of welfare from the individual to the social level? There was an early attempt to extend the scope of welfare economics, led by Abram Bergson, who introduced the idea of a so-called "social welfare function" which is supposed to aggregate individual preferences into social preferences (Bergson 1938). This approach got a major blow from the work of Nobel (1972) laureate economist Kenneth Arrow who looked at the possibility of deriving logically consistent preference orderings of the society in a democratic way (e.g., by majority votes). He formalised his arguments in what is known as the social choice theory, which showed that the democratic rule of majority votes can provide thoroughly inconsistent or illogical preference ordering among, say, some alternative social outcomes. Consider, for example, among three choices, A may be preferred to B by a majority (say, two individuals out of a total three), B may be preferred to C again by a majority, but C is preferred to A by a majority as well, which will not thus yield a consistent social preference ordering of the three choices, although derived from consistent individual orderings.

This pessimistic result is again a reflection of what Sen calls an "informational crisis" of economics in measuring and comparing individual preferences (Sen 1997, pp. 99; Sen 2009, pp. 87–103, 279–82). The subsequent academic discussions around this theory by Sen and other economists had a constructive impact on the theory showing that there can be other approaches to democratically derive preferences for the good of the society at least for a limited range of choices. An individual, instead of acting like what Sen calls a "social moron", has multi-dimensional preferences which reflect, besides self-interest, his ethical values and commitment to his community and society at large. Hence the need for what Sen calls "public reasoning", that is, informed debates and argumentation to sway public opinion in support for such causes as promoting female empowerment or protecting minority rights or various other measures towards establishing a just society. Such "public reasoning" is needed all the more, as Sen argues, on the ground that even consistent preference orderings obtained by majority votes may violate certain minimum ethical standards, such as not protecting the rights of the minorities in society (Sen 1997).

Income inequality

The inability of economic theory to address the welfare implication of income inequality is a serious shortcoming of the discipline. After all, the moral issue regarding capitalism that has always been the subject of the greatest controversy is regarding the inequality that it creates. Adam Smith remarked only casually that where there was wealth, there would be inequality. The issue, however, came to the fore since David Ricardo (1772–1823) concluded, rather dispassionately, about the inevitable impoverishment of the poor and the progressive concentration of wealth. For his detached view, Ricardo was taken to task, among others, by Ruskin who called him a cold-blooded share-broker. That accusation may have been unfair, but even the admirers of Ricardo never suggested that he was a man of passion. Karl Marx (1818–1883), in contrast, was beyond doubt a man of passion, whose mission was to identify the fault of capitalism, place blame and urge change. Although the gloomy predictions of Ricardo or Malthus did not quite materialise, mainly because of the technological developments that would follow, the growth of capitalism has been nevertheless accompanied by increasing inequality and wealth concentration. In his recent bestseller book *Capital in the Twenty-First Century*, French economist Thomas Piketty has convincingly shown, by analysing long-term data, as to why the current capitalist system will lead to an unabated process of wealth concentration (Piketty 2014).

Although modern economic theory has remained as dispassionate as Ricardo, it has sought to explain income distribution in terms of the so-called marginal theory of distribution, which relates the remuneration of factors of production (e.g., land, labour, capital and organisation) to the productivity of those factors. While such a theory of distribution may seem to give some moral legitimacy to the distributional outcome of a market economy, this theory is as far from reality as is the neoclassical model of the competitive market from which it is derived. To illustrate this divergence between theory and reality, Nobel (2008) laureate economist Paul Krugman used a parable which is somewhat as the following (Krugman 1998, p. 54).

Consider two societies: in the first one, everyone makes a living by, say, fishing, while the main source of earning in the second one is gold prospecting. Incomes in the first society will vary to the extent that some people are better at fishing than others and some are willing to work harder than others, but the range of incomes will not be that wide. In contrast, in the second society, a few find rich deposits and become rich, while many find themselves working hard for very little reward. The result will be a very unequal distribution of income which will reflect chance and luck much more than effort and skill. In this society, even among the skilled and industrious prospectors, many will not become rich, while a few become immensely so.

The vast majority of people living especially in today's industrialised countries or in one of the fast-growing developing countries will instinctively agree, whatever may be their ideological leanings, that an economy resembling the second imaginary society is a worse place than one that resembles the first. Yet, most of them will also agree that their own economies have increasingly become more like the unfairly unequal society of prospectors than the benign society of fishermen. Luck surely has a role to play, which is underplayed both by pro-market conservatives who extol the virtues of entrepreneurship and effort and by social democrats who put the blame of inequality entirely on the processes of the market economy. The fact remains that the prevailing global economic scene is one of unprecedented prosperity and inequality. There is also an awareness that the global community faces the moral challenge and has the wherewithal to address the prevailing problem of poverty amidst plenty. In this scenario, the stance of moral neutrality of economics as a discipline would seem all the more incongruous.

Interestingly, in spite of the value-free nature of the neoclassical market theory, there seems to be an implicit moral or ideological bias among the so-called market fundamentalists who interpret this theory as an unconditional support for a free market economy. Replacing the term "capitalism" by "free market economy", or to use the term "rationality" for purely self-interested behaviour, or to define "efficiency" only in a very narrow sense of Pareto optimality in total disregard to distribution may reflect the same bias. Paul Samuelson pointed out how some proponents of the market economy uncritically ascribe the Arrow-Debreau neoclassical general equilibrium model as the modern-day expression of Smith's invisible hand; Smith would be indeed surprised at what is attributed to him today (Samuelson 1993; Kay 2004; p. 197). As for Alfred Marshall, the founder of neoclassical microeconomics, even he could not accept the ruthless amorality of pure laissez faire, while endorsing the view that self-interest and public duty coincided (Robinson 1970, pp. 115–16). In fact, in his own words, Marshall was "passionately concerned with poverty" as quoted by A. C. Pigou, the famous Cambridge economist and a student of Marshall (Pigou 1925, p. 89).

Keynesianism and the welfare state

The welfare implications of neoclassical economic theory, and perhaps economics as a discipline itself, got its severest shock with the onset of the economic recession of the 1930s in the Western capitalist world. It was Maynard Keynes who came to the rescue by convincing governments that the age-old Sage Law of supply creating its own demand does not work in averting economic recessions and that the capitalist system can be saved and near-full employment can be restored by boosting aggregate demand through government spending. As Joan Robinson, one of the foremost left-leaning economists at Cambridge University remarked about Keynes: "Without him economics in the English-speaking world would have been completely discredited and policy would have become the domain of cranks and empirics" (Robinson 1970, p. 114). Although the Keynesian theory was later modified into what is known as post-Keynesian economics to capture new developments in the capitalist system, its links with the modern financial markets remain tenuous at best. The case for public spending has also sometimes been used as what may be called "vulgar Keynesianism", such as the morally repugnant argument that the spending on arms helps to keep the United States and the global economy from falling into recession.

It may be noted that the Keynesian thinking of the welfare state has been challenged by the so-called "public choice" theorist who took a critical view of the capacities and integrity of the democratic governments. This school of thinking, led by Nobel laureate (1986) economist James Buchanan, is based on the assumption that political actors are motivated by self-interest in the same way as economic actors are, thus resulting in adverse outcomes from state policies. The once popular British TV comedy series "Yes Minister" was, in fact, inspired by public choice theory; in the series, both the top bureaucrat and the minister act to maximise their career initially in opposition but eventually in collision. Public choice theories, however, have been largely critiqued for their narrow focus on the self-seeking behaviour of politicians and their ideological bias against state interventions and in favour of a free market economy. Even then, there may be some relevance of these theories in less developed countries with poorly established democratic norms and accountability mechanisms. An ideal state-market mix in those economies depends to a large extent on the integrity and capacity of the governments in implementing policies towards improving the market outcomes.

Policymaking and value judgement

Unlike the theory, studies in applied economics used for policymaking frequently involve ethical issues at least implicitly, which often creates a disconnect between theory and its application. For example, it is now a common practice in compiling economic statistics to estimate "real income" of groups of the population to assess the extent of income inequality; such an exercise implicitly allows measurement and comparison of well-being in terms of material living standards. It is noteworthy that economic theory, from David Ricardo to modern neoclassical economic theory, has been concerned only with what is called *functional* distribution of income, namely, the shares of income that the owners of production factors (e.g., landlords, labourers and capitalists) get because of their ownership of these factors (e.g., in the form of rent, wage and profit). The second idea of income distribution, called the *size* or *personal* income distribution, originates from the works of Vilfredo Pareto in the late nineteenth century and deals with how income is distributed among such units like individuals, family or households. It is the second kind of income distribution that is much more relevant for measuring poverty and inequality and devising policies for the provision of social security measures for the poor. These two different ideas of income distribution again highlight the disconnect between the mainstream economic theorising and applied economic analyses used for policymaking.

In economic policymaking, it is generally recognised that extreme income inequality is undesirable on moral grounds, which makes a case for providing social security to the disadvantaged and for using tax policies as a means of income redistribution. The moral justification for redistributive taxes may also rest on the argument that poverty in a market economy may simply result from economic failure due to bad luck only casually – the "destiny risk" – so that society has a moral duty to provide "insurance" for such failure. The problem, however, arises in determining what should be the yardstick of *fairness* in evaluating income distributional outcomes of a policy. Amartya Sen, for example, has argued that social justice may be judged, not by equality in income, but by equal opportunities for each individual to develop his potential *capabilities* to the fullest extent (Sen 1999, 2009).

The moral case for income redistribution is, of course, mixed with economic arguments, made rightly or wrongly, such as whether providing social security for the poor adversely affects their incentives for participating in the labour market or to what extent there is a disincentive effect of high taxes on the entrepreneurial rich. On the other hand, inequality may also be considered to be a hindrance to economic development by adversely affecting social cohesion or by stymying the drive of the poor to improve their lot.

The political debates between the conservative right and the social democratic left in the Western capitalist countries is largely couched in terms of their respective assessment of these economic consequences of redistributive policies, although such debates are more often driven by ideological beliefs than empirical evidence. For example, one extreme form of the ideas on the right took the form of so-called "supply-side economics", alternatively known as *Reaganomics*, that claimed with little evidence that allowing large tax concessions for the wealthy at the cost of reducing welfare spending for the poor can help the poor by boosting economic growth and employment creation and can even increase the total tax revenues (the so-called Laffer curve). The intellectual grounding for lowering the tax rates for the rich was provided by the Nobel (1999) economist Robert Mundell, whose advocates then rallied under the banner of supply-side economics and won over many right-leaning politicians and policymakers in the United States, Britain and elsewhere, while drawing the scorns of more progressive economists. Economists can no doubt usefully contribute to such debates, but this alone cannot settle the central question of redistribution, namely, what is a society's obligation to its poor? The answer to this will depend on the value judgement about what is fair and just, which cannot be resolved only by assessing the economic impact of redistributive policies.

Besides the issue of income distribution, there are other serious ethical issues to be resolved. It is well recognised that the market is an amoral and often cruelly capricious master. To "humanise" the system, any responsible government has to take action in areas where the market does a poor job – such as providing social security for the poor, investing in basic health and education, protecting the environment and providing many kinds of public goods. As back as in 1920, Artur Pigou (Keynes' professor at Cambridge) introduced in his book *The Economics of Welfare* the idea of "polluter pays" principle to make firms that create pollution accountable for the consequences of their decision for society. In today's world with growing concern about the adverse effects of climate change, there is a demand from environmentalists to restructure the tax systems so that the prices of products should reflect the damage that their production causes to the environment. Public provision of universal basic healthcare and education, ensuring human security and action for the protection of environment are increasingly being recognised as preconditions for sustained equitable growth in developing countries, such as envisioned in the United Nations' Sustainable Development Goals (the SDGs). Economic theory provides very little guidance for the governments in deciding about priorities in allocating public funds towards performing such a variety of public welfare activities – policies that involve not only many trade-offs but also beneficial synergies.

Money as a measuring rod of value

The size and growth of gross national product (GDP) in per capita terms is the single most accepted measure of the economic performance of a country and across countries. There are, however, many serious shortcomings of GDP as representing the well-being of a nation, some of which are well-known but others less discussed. One of these less discussed shortcomings is that GDP is estimated on the basis of market prices, which are a reflection of society's preferences for the marketed goods and services, but only with the given distribution of income. Had the distribution been different, the price configuration (along with the resource allocation for production) could be very different, resulting in different estimates of the size and growth of GDP.

The most striking example of the price mechanism not doing a good job is perhaps provided by such precious stones like gold or diamond, which not only happen to be perhaps the least "useful" among all minerals, but also the mining of which causes huge environmental damage. But as long as the market demand for gold and other precious stones remain as it is, the prices will remain high because of the limited supply and high cost of production. In a film made by the renowned Indian film director Satyajit Ray, a poor office clerk came across a stone that had the magical power of turning any metal by touch into gold (the mythical philosopher's stone, called *Parash Pathar* in Bengali, which is also the title of the film). The clerk eventually got disillusioned by his newly gotten wealth from selling gold and wanted to dispose of the stone when the story broke out in the news media. The entire city of Kolkata went into a frenzy with people trying to sell whatever gold items they had and the gold market collapsing overnight. Fortunately for the gold business, the stone lost its magical power and disappeared. The story of course follows the basic principle of economics that anything in unlimited supply has no market price and is not considered an "economic" good. But it also reveals the less obvious fact that the high market price of gold partly derives from its "socially constructed" demand for ornaments (and, thereby, as a store of value) and not for any of its intrinsic value (unlike the air that we breathe, which is also not an economic good).

The same income distributional bias of markets is the reason why there are objections on moral grounds against privatisation of, say, water supply, which may limit the poor's access to safe water. In fact, the debate about the privatisation of water supply is an example of how advocacy of the market economy can clash with moral values. As water has increasingly become a scarce resource in many countries of the world, there are strong business lobbies for making water a marketable product; even many economists have also argued in favour of privatising the water market. Against this, there has been civic activism worldwide against "commodifying" water on the ethical ground that access to potable water is a fundamental human right, a view that has been endorsed by the UN General Assembly in 2010 by an overwhelming majority of votes, albeit with less enthusiasm from most of the industrialised countries, 41 of them abstaining from voting.

Another problem with using the market price as the measuring rod of value is that it tends to ignore or undervalue things that contribute to the quality of life but are not amenable to valuation in monetary terms. Spending on a pricey non-essential medical test or cigarette advertisement contributes to GDP while the health benefits from a clean environment do not, at least not directly. Economics is least useful in measuring many non-market aspects of human well-being such as the risk to the life of workers posed by unsafe factory environment, the aesthetic value of natural beauty being diminished by environmental degradation, the psychic costs of forced migration caused by climate change, the cost of gender discrimination or the welfare of the future generation threatened by climate change. Economists have shown ingenuity in including some of these in GDP estimation or policy evaluation in some roundabout ways, which are not often very convincing. For example, a time discount rate is used while doing cost-benefit analysis of public investment projects that may have, say, a 30-year lifetime, but the use of such a discount rate for a project that will entail environmental costs for generations to come has dubious moral validity. According to Nicholas Stern (2013), a former Chief Economist of the World

Bank, many economic models grossly underestimate the risk of unmanaged climate change "because of the assumptions built into the economic modelling on growth, damages and risks" (Stern 2013). The controversy around measuring the costs of climate change has been rekindled by the awarding of the 2018 Nobel Prize to William Nordhaus for his work on the effect of climate change on future Global GDP.

The tradition in economics to exclude or undervalue the non-materialistic and non-market aspects of well-being goes back to the late nineteenth century when Alfred Marshall, the founder of neoclassical economics, declared the correct focus of economics to be the "attainment and ... use of material requisites of well-being", or, as his student, Arthur Pigou, put it, "the part of social welfare that can be brought directly or indirectly in relation with the measuring rod of money". Marshall also casually suggested in a footnote of his seminal book *Principles of Economics* (1890) that unpaid household work could be left out of economic activities, which is now regarded by some economists as a value judgement, especially from a gender perspective. While the scope of activities to be included in economic accounting has widened to a large extent since then, it seems likely that economists today still treat things which cannot be easily measured as if they matter less.

Ironically, however, economic cost-benefit calculations may have been overextended to explain such non-market familial behaviour as the decision to marry or divorce or parents' choice about the number of children they want or the amount of investment they would like to make on them. Led by Gary Becker, the Nobel (1992) laureate economist of Chicago University, such an approach to familial decision-making based solely on cool economic calculations has been criticised by many for ignoring basic human emotions like parents' love for their children and the joy of raising a family. The works of many great literary authors like Jane Austen or Leo Tolstoy show how economic calculations may be mixed with other emotions in family decision-making. A recent book co-authored by Gary Morson and Morton Schapiro, a literary critic and an economist, respectively, refers to a less-known book of Adam Smith, *The Theory of Moral Sentiments*, and contends that a few decades later Jane Austen invented her groundbreaking method of novelistic narration in order to give life to the empathy that Smith believed essential to humanity (Morson and Morton 2017).

The question may be raised as to why, in doing policy analysis, economists cannot stick to purely value-free objective analyses by using the tools of their trade and leave for the politicians to choose among the policy outcomes according to their value judgement. This is neither possible nor desirable for several reasons. First, policy analyses are often so complex that economists have to fill in gaps with ethical contents before

they present their results in an easily digestible way for the consideration of the political decision-makers. Judgements have to be made, for
example, about how to deal with various externalities like industrial pollution, or how to measure various non-tangible costs or benefits, or what
indices of cost of living are best suitable for estimating "real incomes", or
what discount rates and income distributional weights to use in the social
cost-benefit analysis of public investment projects. Second, some ethical
considerations may go into policy analyses while prodding the policymakers to seek answers to the right questions. Third, choosing the right topics
for economic analysis, such as the impact analysis for various poverty
interventions, has to be often guided by economists' own notions of fairness and justice. Finally, economists may choose to play the role of public
intellectuals to sway public opinion in favour of policies that they support
from a moral standpoint. While economists are likely to have a diversity
of views, they can help inform public discourses on contentious issues.
The US magazine *Newsweek* had regular columns during 1966–1981 on
contemporary economic topics written by the two giants of the economic
profession, Milton Friedman (1976 Nobel laureate) who had passionate
beliefs in free markets and Paul Samuelson (the first American to win
Economics Nobel in 1976) who had more liberal views regarding the market versus state interventions.

In lieu of a conclusion

Economists may do better by including in their analyses an improved understanding of the complexity of human behaviour, for example, by drawing
from new ideas developed in neuroscience and experimental psychology;
they also need to allow more scope for ethical judgements in their choice of
topics for inquiry, in their methodological approaches and in drawing policy
conclusions. Even if the motivation for monetary gains may be the dominant behavioural trait in economic dealings, there are instances in which
the separation of self-interest from other traits including ethical values is
less than straightforward. It also needs to be recognised that all market
transactions are not necessarily *fair*, or even welfare-enhancing. Moreover,
an understanding of how social value system, preferences and aspirations
are formed may give economists better clues and insights in devising policies that may contribute towards social well-being. The need for interdisciplinary approaches in economic policy analyses and for making moral
judgements may become more compelling as society and economy evolve
in response to climate change or the onset of pandemics like Covid-19, and
as new technological breakthroughs take place, such as in artificial intel-
ligence and the emergence of social media platforms. Simply put, without

losing the analytical rigour, which is the hallmark of the discipline, economics needs to be broader in order to be better.

Notes

1 For an overview of the relations between economics and ethics, see Sen, Amartya (1987), Hausman and McPherson (1996), Buchanan (1985) and Hamlin (1986). For discussions on some of the related issues particularly in the context of developing countries, see also Basu (2011).
2 The term "econ" has been used in the recent literature on behavioural economics; more traditional literature used the term *homo economicus*.
3 Interview with the *Brain World* magazine, July 2020.
4 Reprinted in Krugman, P. (1998), pp. 79.
5 For a detailed discussion on this from a different set of perspectives, see Hausman and McPherson (1996), pp. 9–16.

References

Akerlof, G. (1970). "The markets for lemons: Qualitative uncertainty and the market mechanism". *Quarterly Journal of Economics*, Vol. 84, pp. 488–500.
Bardhan, P. and Udry, C. (1999). *Development Microeconomics*. Oxford: Oxford University Press.
Basu, Kaushik. (2011). *Beyond the Invisible Hand: Groundwork for a New Economics*. Princeton, NJ: Princeton University Press.
Bergson, A. (1938). "A reformulation of certain aspects of welfare economics". *Quarterly Journal of Economics*, Vol. 52, pp. 30–4.
Bhagwati, Jagdish. (2004). *In Defence of Globalization*. New Delhi: Oxford University Press.
Buchanan, Allen E. (1985). *Ethics, Efficiency and the Market*. Totowa, NJ: Rowman and Allanheld.
Hausman, Daniel M. and McPherson, Michael S. (1996). *Economic Analysis and Moral Philosophy*. Cambridge, UK: Cambridge University Press.
Hamlin, Alan. (1986). *Ethics, Economics and the State*. New York: St. Martin's Press.
Hicks, John. (1969). *The Theory of Economic History*. Oxford, UK: Oxford University Press.
Hirsch, F. (1977). *Social Limits to Growth*. London: Routledge and Kegan Paul.
Kay, J. (2004). *Culture and Prosperity: Why Some Nations Are Rich but Most Remain Poor*. New York: HarperCollins.
Krugman, P. (1998). *The Accidental Theorist*. New York: W. W. Norton & Company.
Lowenstein, R. (1995). *Buffet: The Making of an American Capitalist*. New York: Random House.
McMillan, John. (2002). *Reinventing the Bazaar: A Natural History of Markets*. New York: W. W. Norton & Company.
Morishima, M. (1982). *Why Has Japan 'Succeeded': Western Technology and Japanese Ethos*. Cambridge: Cambridge University Press.

Morson, G. S. and Morton Schapiro. (2017). *Cents and Sensibility: What Economists Can Learn from the Humanities*. Princeton, NJ: Princeton University Press.

Piketty, Thomas. (2014). *Capital in the Twenty-First Century*. Cambridge, MA: The Belknap Press of Harvard University Press.

Pigou, A. C. (ed.). (1925). *Memorials of Alfred Marshall*. London: Macmillan.

Robinson, Joan. (1970). *Freedom and Necessity: An Introduction to the Study of Society*. London: George Allen & Unwin.

Samuelson, Paul A. (1993). "Altruism as a problem involving group versus individual selection in economics and biology". *American Economic Review*, Vol. 83, No. 2 (May), pp. 1943–8.

Samuelson, Paul A. (1958). "An exact consumption-loan model of interest with or without the social contrivance of overlapping generations". *Journal of Political Economy*, Vol. 66, pp. 518–22.

Sen, Amartya K. (1984). "The profit motive". In Sen, Amartya K. *Resources, Values and Development*. New Delhi: Oxford University Press.

Sen, Amartya K. (1987). *On Ethics and Economics*. Oxford: Basil Blackwell.

Sen, Amartya K. (1997). *Choice, Welfare and Measurement*. Cambridge, MA: Harvard University Press.

Sen, Amartya K. (1999). *Development as Freedom*. Oxford: Oxford University Press.

Sen, Amartya K. (2009). *The Idea of Justice*. London, England: Allen Lane Penguin Books.

Stern, Nicholas. (2013). "The structure of economic modelling of the potential impacts of climate change: Grafting underestimation of risk into already narrow science models". *Journal of Economic Literature*, Vol. 51, No. 3, pp. 838–59.

Stiglitz, Joseph E. (2002). *Globalization and its Discontents*. New York: W. W. Norton & Company.

Tirole, Jean. (2016). *Economics for the Common Good*. Princeton, NJ: Princeton University Press.

Winter Jr., S. G. (1969). "A simple remark on the second optimality theorem of welfare economics". *Journal of Economic Theory*, Vol. 1, No. 1, pp. 99–103.

4 Institutions, morality norms and development

Introduction: the moral boundaries of markets

Economic development is accompanied by a process of institutional transformation in which traditional production technologies, local knowledge and informal behavioural norms are replaced or complemented by improved technologies, modern know-how and formal regulatory enforcement of business dealings. The less developed countries provide interesting case studies of how this transformation may take place in different ways, sometimes by creating frictions and undermining the impact of development interventions, but sometimes resulting in beneficial socio-economic dynamics. Development economics can benefit much from a better understanding of how the so-called "informal economy" based on traditionally evolved behavioural norms interact with the introduction of a modern market economy with formal regulation.

All markets, in fact, operate within the boundaries set by the complex institutions of economic, social and political life with formal regulation, implicit rules and norms, and mechanisms of cooperation and coordination. In their seminal book on the neoclassical theory of general equilibrium, Kenneth Arrow and Frank Hahn ask the question: "What will an economy motivated by individual greed ... look like?" and agree with the common-sense answer: there will be chaos (Arrow and Hahn 1971, p. vii). According to Arrow, "the model of the *laissez faire* world of total self-interest would not survive for ten minutes; its actual working depends on an intricate network of reciprocal obligations, even among competing firms and individuals" (Arrow 1978). Back in 1739, the English Philosopher David Hume observed in his book *Treatise on Human Nature* that commerce and business can flourish only on a relationship of trust and honouring of contract. In the modern-day discussions on economic development, there is now a growing recognition among economists of the importance of the so-called "social capital", consisting of mutual obligation, trust, norms and customs,

DOI: 10.4324/9781003241775-4

as the "infrastructure" in which markets are embedded. As Kaushik Basu, a former Chief Economist at the World Bank, observes: while it is obvious that an individual's behaviour is shaped by these social norms, "what is less obvious is that an individual's adherence to certain social norms may be a *necessary* element in many economic models" (Basu 1997, p. 8).

In every society, ethical norms evolve to set the boundaries for the otherwise self-regarding materialism of the market economy. An ethical element of trust enters in some measure into every business contract, without which no market could function. Arrow used the extreme example of the service of a doctor, who has to be trusted by his patients. Basu (1997, pp. 9–10) uses an example from the day-to-day urban life, similar to the following: Why do you not walk away without paying the fare after a rickshaw ride on a lonely street? If you argue that you do not do so because the rickshaw-puller happens to be physically strong enough to forcibly extract fare from you, then why does he not attempt to extract the fare a second time after you have paid his correct fare? These are matters of common values and norms in a society that underlie the working of the market economy. And it is not adequate to argue that there are legal enforcement mechanisms such as police and courts, since these are themselves institutions that cannot perform without some minimum ethical standards.

Nobel laureate (1993) economist Douglas North, who pioneered the field of institutional economics, explains how cultural and social values affect "transaction costs" of economic dealings and can constrain or facilitate economic transformation. Institutions create the incentive structure in an economy, such as for unproductive activities like rent-seeking or for entrepreneurial innovations; the way economic agents take advantage of opportunities provided within an institutional framework in turn will change and gradually alter the institutional framework, for better or worse. According to North, economists' "preoccupation with rational choice and efficient market hypotheses have blinded" them to "complexity of human motivation" and limited their understanding of not only why institutions exist but also how they influence outcomes (North 1990, pp. 110–11). It is said that, before taking a consulting job overseas, Professor North insisted on spending at least six months in a country, absorbing its belief systems and its organisation and institutional framework before offering his advice.[1]

Evolution of cooperative behaviour

Economists have often struggled to explain why there is so much more cooperative behaviour in the world than the pursuit of self-interest would imply. Cooperative behaviour is found to be quite strong and provide the basis for organisations in the economy. The introduction of the so-called game theory, which was pioneered by John Nash (portrayed in the movie *Beautiful Mind*) and which has a wide-ranging application both in evolutionary biology and economics, can provide insights on such behaviour of reciprocity that may evolve over time from the experience gained from interactive behaviour.

The most widely used example in this context is known as the Prisoner's Dilemma problem. It describes a situation in which two persons take decisions independently of each other knowing that the outcome for each one will depend on the action of both. Both can gain more by acting in good faith of mutual cooperation than without such cooperation. But the situation is complicated by the possibility that one will cooperate and the other will not, in which case the former gets the worst deal while the other gains the most. Without mutual trust, each of them in such a situation is likely to take the safe course of non-cooperation, suspecting that the other may outwit him by defecting and taking advantage of his offer of cooperation. This example of the game theory thus explains how the gains of cooperation cannot be reaped by unilateral "rational" behaviour. Maximising self-interest in such a case is not of course straightforward. Each player chooses to go for the most he can get, taking into account that the other player may not cooperate, which is known as the "maximum of the minimum" strategy.

But if the game is repeated over and over again, each player can gather experience about the reactive behaviour of the other. In an experimental set-up, with numerous repeated rounds of the game, a strategy of reciprocity (or, one can call less generously a tit-for-tat) is found to be the winner by yielding the highest average gains per round of the game; the strategy is to reward cooperation of the other in the previous round by offering cooperation in the current round and punishing defection by defection in the same way. This is one way of explaining how cooperative behaviour may result from the expectations of reciprocity and may eventually become a social norm. But, while economists feel comfortable with the assumption of self-regarding calculative human behaviour, other social scientists may very well like to find explanations for such cooperative behaviour in other human traits like altruism, cooperative instinct, trust and various community-specific characteristics. In his groundbreaking work on the evolution of cooperation, Robert Axelrod, a political scientist, used the game theory framework to show how reciprocity interacts with a range of other social factors to evolve into a stable behavioural norm of cooperation (Axelrod and Dion 1988).

There are even other ways of looking at the historical roots of how cooperative behaviour evolved in different communities. Some recent studies have found links between historical agricultural practices in various regions of the world with community attitudes towards cooperation. Some studies have found that cooperative behaviour is more common in the rice-growing areas of China, where rice production was dependent on the availability of water for irrigation, than in other parts of the country. The reverse may be true of Bangladesh (the original East Bengal), which historically attracted migrants from outside because of the lure of easy rice cultivation, entirely dependent at that time on monsoon rains and broadcast method of cultivation (that is, by throwing seeds on moist land without the need for seedbeds, transplantation and irrigation). One may wonder whether this has anything to do with the fact that microcredit, which essentially supports individual enterprises, has become so widespread in Bangladesh, while the once-heralded Comilla model of farmers' cooperatives of the 1960s could not eventually sustain due to alleged elite capture and conflict of interest among farmer groups (Khan 1979). Whatever may be the historical origins of cooperative behaviour, economic development all over the world may now need increasingly more cooperative arrangements in many areas ranging from optimal use of scarce land and water resources to sustainable urbanisation and environmental protection.

The norms of civic behaviour of city-dwellers, such as obeying traffic rules or proper disposal of litter and household waste, affect the quality of urban life and liveability of cities, which are related to economic development. The prospect of the habit-forming nature of such civic behaviour can again be explained by the application of the so-called "Prisoner's Dilemma" problem discussed earlier. In this problem, city-dwellers will prefer a situation in which everyone abides by the rules, since they all benefit from a clean city or a city where traffic rules are followed, but each of them may be tempted to cheat the system in the expectation that others will not; the result is widespread non-compliance, which is not the preferred outcome. However, there may be a learning process in which everyone may eventually realise that cooperating with each other in observing the rules instead of acting for short-run self-interest (a "rational" behaviour in theory) will be in the long-run interest of all. In the economic literature on "public good", however, one would treat this as the so-called "free-rider" problem that can be solved either by excluding the benefit to those who shirk their responsibility (not feasible in the examples cited here) or by imposing a municipal tax on all households to cover the cost of door-to-door collection of waste (may not be a desirable option for the taxpayers) or by strictly enforcing the rules (for which the city authorities may not have enough capacity). In comparison, the establishment of behavioural norms of cooperation through a learning process as described above is a more ethical and desirable goal to achieve.[2]

The learning process for cooperative behaviour in a "Prisoner's Dilemma"–like situation described above is often facilitated by community initiatives, such as for waste management and cleanliness in the neighbour-hood. Such initiatives can have a snowball effect as was once shown in the case of the Indian city, Kolkata. There are also examples of initiatives taken by businessmen and traders on their own for fair business practices that will benefit the business community as a whole, such as abstaining from marketing harmful products or not engaging in harmful price com-petition. In Vietnam, there was not much of a market regulatory frame-work when market-oriented reforms were introduced in the early 1990s for encouraging the growth of private businesses. The business communities themselves framed rules for self-regulation such as regarding fair competi-tion, product standards and market integration through exchange of infor-mation. The subsequent success of the Vietnamese economy owed to a great extent to the way the businessmen and entrepreneurs could create the rules of the game themselves and relied on their own devices (McMillan 2002, p. 58). However, the capacity for cooperative behaviour may vary across societies depending on the historical roots of how social norms evolved over time.

One of the two recipients of the Nobel Prize in economics in 2009, Elinor Ostrom was the first ever woman to receive this prize; her works as a political economist was mainly based on case studies from develop-ing countries providing insights into how communities can manage local common resources. For example, she studied the management of the irri-gation systems in Nepal to show how development projects can perform poorly when implemented by a central bureaucracy without local knowl-edge about the communities that are to be benefited by the project. She found an apparently paradoxical phenomenon: the large irrigation projects of the central government, with modern dams and canals often built with the support of foreign donors, seem to work poorly compared with the tra-ditional rudimentary system of irrigation built and maintained by farmers themselves. Why?

An irrigation system, whether built with mud (as in the traditional system) or with bricks and concrete (as in the modern projects), essentially needs regular maintenance of the canals, so that the water diverted by the dam can flow from the upstream all the way to the farmlands that are at the far ends of the canals. The farming communities worked out a system of coopera-tion, in which the farmers downstream offered their labour to construct the dams and the canals in exchange for assistance by the farmers upstream to maintain the channels afterwards. While the details of the arrangement of this division of labour may differ from one community to another, the basic principle is the same. When the modern system was built, not much attention was given to the maintenance of the canals, while the traditional system of cooperation among farmers was also gone. The supposedly more efficient and cost-effective modern irrigation projects became dysfunctional with the eventual clogging of the canals.[3]

There are several lessons to be learnt from Ostrom's above analysis of how the designing and implementation of development projects can go wrong. The civil servants and donor agencies are more concerned with the construction of "prestige" infrastructure projects than with their eventual maintenance; they also tend to ignore the needs and incentives of the local communities. For the civil servants, being involved in the construction phase of such high-profile projects are more rewarding than the more arduous and less glamorous tasks of supervising the routine work of maintenance in remote localities. The donor agency officials are more interested in meeting their spending targets and completing the projects than in evaluating the results. All this points to the need for involving the local communities in the designing and maintenance of such projects; in the case of the Nepalese irrigation projects, it is the farmers who would be most interested in maintaining an irrigation system once it is built. In Bangladesh, an evaluation by the World Bank in respect of the rehabilitation of local-level projects of flood management, drainage and river erosion control found that the original purpose of the projects was endorsed by more than 80 percent of the people in the respective localities, but only one out of the 35 projects could be successfully rehabilitated; the neglect of the details of local circumstances and poor maintenance were found to be the main cause of failure (Mahmud 2002, p. 14).

Measuring development

Among various economic statistics and indicators, gross domestic product (GDP) is perhaps the one that features most frequently in public economic discourses; it also often arouses much confusion and passionate political debates. Much of the controversies surrounding GDP (in common with other national income measures like gross national income [GNI][4]) arise from the varying perceptions about what GDP stands for. When politicians claim about good economic performance, they talk about growth in GDP. The critics of the concept of GDP point to its well-known shortcomings: it ignores non-income aspects of well-being, it does not take into account the environmental damage caused by economic activities and it tends to ignore or undervalue things that contribute to the quality of life but are not amenable to valuation in monetary terms. The estimation of GDP is based on market prices that reflect society's preferences only at the given distribution of purchasing power in the economy, which is often highly unequal.

Much of the confusion arises from the fact that GDP is a measure of material output (and services), not well-being. The first national accounts were estimated by Simon Kuznets immediately before World War II; it was primarily intended to provide a framework for managing the resources available to the wartime economy. James Meade and Richard Stone of Cambridge University, under the tutelage of Maynard Keynes, produced the first official and comprehensive set of national accounts; that framework still provides the basis of the modern national accounting system (Kay 2004, pp. 38–40). Kuznets, Meade and Stone all won economics Nobel Prize, respectively, in 1971, 1977 and 1984. The internationally agreed upon standard set of recommendations about how to compile national income estimates, called the System of National Accounts (SNAs), are revised from time to time to fine-tune the estimates in light of the changes in the structure of the global economy and by finding ways of imputing monetary values to items that previously remained outside the national accounts (e.g., scientific discoveries or works of art).

Spotting signs of development

Economic development can be viewed from different perspectives, but the overriding theme is one of improving human well-being. Given the various shortcomings of GDP even as a measure of material living standards, let alone of well-being, there have been attempts to find other measures of economic development. The idea of gauging economic development by indicators other than GDP, such as the *Human Development Index*, or measures that reflect footprints of environmental damage, has grown out of the dissatisfaction with GDP. There is scope for economists to continue to refine and develop such various indicators of development, each of which has its merits and shortcomings, but is helpful in highlighting various aspects of economic development. In doing so, they need to be, however, wary about new ideas such as ranking of countries by the so-called "happiness index"; the way such indices are usually estimated has little support even from the studies on experimental psychology (Kahneman 2011, pp. 391–7).

When a visitor from a less developed country arrives at an affluent or a relatively more advanced country, he can see the difference instantly from casual observation; he does not have to check with the publications of the World Bank or of the UN Development Programme (UNDP) to find the relative ranking of that country in terms of per capita GDP or the *Human Development Index*. Knowing what those apparently visible signs of development are may sometimes help one to have a *reality check* on the claims of his government regarding economic development and may also reveal some missing elements of development in his own country. After all, a student of economics, doing elaborate statistical exercises in measuring and comparing economic development across countries, should not be accused of missing things which even the untrained eyes of a visitor can easily spot. Leaving aside a visitor's first general impression about how orderly the immigration procedures are at the entry airport, the signs of development will be obviously more detectable in the metropolitan areas, since that is where economic development has the most impact. As an illustration, the following could perhaps serve as a tentative list of items:

- The quality of public transport; whether a time schedule is maintained and passengers get in and out at fixed stops and not in the middle of the road; the very look of the vehicles.
- How orderly is the traffic; compliance to traffic rules and the extent of sound pollution through honking; whether roads are well maintained and there are not many potholes; how much priority is given to pedestrian facilities, and the extent to which the sidewalks of main roads are crowded by hawkers and vendors and make-shift shops.
- The quality of tap water, the standards of food safety, the efficacy of the waste management system and the availability of public toilets.
- The availability and quality of public libraries.
- The degree of etiquette and politeness people show in public places.
- The aesthetic beauty of the main riverside or the lakeside that grows naturally with the development of urban amenities, as distinct from any artificial beautification projects that more often than not give a lacklustre look because of poor maintenance.

If the visitor happens to venture into the countryside, there may be a few visible signs of development, such as the outward look of the homesteads, the availability of power supply or the nature of agricultural implements on farmlands. Also, in the above list, there may be other candidates for inclusion, but there is also no point in lengthening the list if a single indicator can represent many other hidden indicators. Notice that we have not included such indicators as the degree of air pollution or the number of pavement dwellers, since there may not be a regular pattern to match with economic development (the San Francisco area in the United States may have more pavement dwellers than in many cities in poor countries).

To an economist, such a heterogeneous mix of indicators may not have much meaning in explaining development, since these may be variously related to development either as the ingredients or the results of development or merely as associated with development with apparently no causal significance. Even though these indicators may reveal various aspects of development, such as the state capacity to provide civic amenities, the quality of investment in human and physical capital and the behavioural norms of people in their civic life, an economist is unlikely to be much interested in things like these that cannot be reduced to measurable indices. Moreover, most of these indicators are in the nature of "public goods" and not directly related to households' private incomes as reflected in their living standards – the indicator of primary interest to economists in measuring economic development.

One may still wonder why these apparently visible signs are so systematically and stubbornly related to economic prosperity and whether these indicate some underlying broader socio-cultural settings into which the functioning of the economies is embedded. After all, economists have not yet got much of a clue in explaining how a present-day less developed country could become an industrialised one, beyond, for example, prescribing that it should follow the example of the East Asian miracle economies; which is like saying that, if you want to play good cricket, play like Sachin Tendulkar. Among economies with significantly large population, South Korea is the only country to have graduated from a less developed country to an industrialised one in the post-World War II period (most recently, Chile and Colombia have also been included among the list of the industrialised or the so-called OECD countries, but they started with a higher economic base). Even among those East Asian miracle stories, there is not any unique model to follow. While South Korean industrialisation was mostly through the rise of state-supported big industrial conglomerates, Taiwan's emphasis was on the growth of small and medium enterprises. Governments have little alternative but to follow an experimental approach to the implementation of development policies – a principle that is expressed well by former Chinese leader Deng Xiaoping's oft-quoted dictum to "cross the river by feeling for the stones", or as implied by Nobel (1987) economist Robert Solow's comment in this context: "You have to grope your way".[5]

Coming back to spotting the signs of development, a discerning economist, unlike the casual tourist, will be interested to delve deeper to find causal connections. He may heed the advice given by Douglas North mentioned earlier and would possibly stay longer in the country, if he is to give any policy advice to the government of that country. Which signs will he be looking for to find what makes the economy work the way it does – or does not?

He may note how much time, trouble and speed money (that is, bribe) it takes to get even a simple thing done, like getting a permit to stay longer than originally permitted by his visa. Are things done more through personal connections or according to impersonal rules that do not discriminate between the elite and the ordinary citizens? He may be trying to assess the quality of human resources and the education system as reflected, say, in the number of expatriates in technical and managerial positions, and in the quality of the college and university graduates; do many of these educated young seek jobs abroad, which may be a sign that the education they have received has not much contributed to their employability at home and also may indicate their lack of confidence in the country's economic future. Are there many large-scale infrastructure projects of only "prestige value" but not well-planned to serve their purpose? Even amid a general environment of deficient governance, do there still exist at least some government agencies that are well-resourced and professionally competent and able to identify problems, work out solutions and act promptly? Such dynamic agencies can potentially set examples for the work culture in other agencies, or at least can act as agents of change in their spheres of activity.

Overall, one may be looking for a system of governance in which there is vertical mechanisms for *accountability* of the government functionaries at each layer of administration, as well as horizontal coordination across various government agencies. The opposite extreme is perhaps an unwieldy leviathan-like governance structure in which even the well-meaning and honest actors feel alienated. Although aware of the pitfalls of the system, they are unable to do anything about it on their own like the characters in Kafka's novels.

Governance and norms of morality

In the contemporary literature on economic development, there is a growing recognition of the links between the prospects of economic growth of a country with the quality of its governance. This new emphasis on "governance", originating mostly from the Bretton Woods institutions, can benefit from the earlier literature on the "social capital" and the institutional development of a society mentioned above. The usual policy advice is mainly to do with devising and enforcing appropriate policy reforms aimed at building business-friendly institutions, such as to reduce corruption, maintain the basic law and order, ensure property rights or to address the bureaucratic hurdles, all of which could reduce the currently high cost of doing business. However, these procedural and enforcement problems in the formal governance structure are only one side of the coin; on the other side are the issues of behavioural norms and ethical standards prevalent among various stakeholder groups in society. Administrative reforms towards enforcing accountability and reducing corruption among government functionaries are less likely to succeed without an understanding of how incentives for deviant behaviour arise and how behavioural norms are formed. This is also true regarding attempts towards preventing unholy collusion among market regulators and unscrupulous businessmen when such collusive behaviour has already become the norm.

The problem can in fact be more serious than what appears at a first glance. Any widespread unethical behaviour is obviously difficult to address because of the sheer magnitude of the problem. A less obvious phenomenon is that, beyond a certain tipping point, the prevalence of such behaviour becomes self-reinforcing and continuously erodes ethical standards. Consider, for example, the spread of the culture of bribery in government offices. When bribery is not so widespread, the individual official's financial benefit from bribes may not be worth the cost in terms of searching for a willing client and the risk of being reported and punished, even leaving aside the psychological cost of a guilty conscience. But this cost-benefit calculus of bribery may be reversed when such practice is so widespread that it becomes a behavioural norm with a lesser feeling of guilt while the risk of detection and punishment is also much less. The important lesson from this analysis is that unless an anti-corruption campaign is of a scale that can bring the prevalence of corruption well within the tipping point, corruption will again spread as soon as the campaign ends. If the campaign is prolonged enough, there will ultimately be even less need for punitive actions as new norms of ethical standards take hold, thus favourably altering the initial cost-benefit calculations of corruption along with the tipping point in favour of the self-correcting mechanism. The ethical standards are not thus given, but respond to the timing and extent of the application of formal deterrence mechanisms. A similar analysis by Mahmud and Osmani (2017, pp. 44–8) shows how, in a mature microfinance system as in Bangladesh, coercion in loan repayment can be gradually relaxed as the cost-benefit calculations of borrowers for repayment default are altered by habit formation and establishment of social norms of repayment.

There are numerous other areas of the functioning of the economy in less developed countries where legal and regulatory enforcement mechanisms interact with the evolution of moral standards. The lax enforcement of tax laws, for example, leads to a culture of tax evasion, while weak loan recovery mechanisms of the banking system may lead to a culture of wilful repayment default, resulting in huge portfolios of non-performing loans. Then there are unscrupulous businesses thriving in an environment of lax regulation, and in the process, driving out the honest ones. The result, for example, is factories that disregard safety and labour standards or markets inundated by sub-standard drugs and adulterated foods posing grievous threats to public health.

In the absence of enforcement of regulation regarding product standards, the problem of marketing harmful products can be self-reinforcing for a more serious reason beyond the lack of moral standards of traders and businessmen. This is explained by the theory of market with imperfect information for which George Akerlof won Nobel Prize in economics in 2001 (Akerlof 1970). This theory breaks away from the traditional neoclassical market theory by assuming that buyers have much less knowledge than sellers about the quality of the products – an assumption that applies to a wide variety of marketed products in less developed countries. In such a market, even if there are mostly honest sellers to start with, they will be increasingly driven out of the market by dishonest sellers. In the case of food adulteration, for example, this happens in the following way: since the buyers offer a price with the knowledge that there is a probability – however small to start with – of getting adulterated food, this price will be a good incentive for the sellers of adulterated food, but less so for the honest sellers. So more dishonest sellers will enter the market and the buyers will know by experience of a higher probability of getting the adulterated food and will offer even less price; the process will continue until only adulterated food is supplied in the market unless the regulatory authorities start enforcing laws to punish food adulterators.

The governance dysfunction in the less developed countries may also manifest in many kinds of malfeasant rent-seeking activities, such as involving in share market scams or large-scale wilful loan repayment defaults or money laundering resulting in capital flight or unlawful grabbing of common property resources. Such malfeasant activities, which may do great harm to the pace and quality of economic growth, are perpetrated by the influential elite who benefit from a culture of patronage politics; as such, these activities do not fit into the category of behavioural norms among large sections of people discussed above. Modern institutional economics has advanced some hypotheses in this regard.

First, if the leading political and economic entrepreneurs are the beneficiaries of the prevailing system of governance dysfunction, they have little incentive to change the system; which is why a big jolt is needed to correct the moral compass of the system. Second, effective governance reforms seek to find entry points in which there are unexploited potentials for all stakeholders to gain from win–win compromises, such as mandatory enforcement of factory environment may lead to productivity gains that can benefit both labourers and the factory owners, but the space for such compromises becomes limited since it does not apply to interest groups who continue to thrive by unlawful rent-seeking activities outside the normal functioning of a well-regulated market economy. Third, a government embarking on a simultaneous campaign of law enforcement and moral suasion needs to have the confidence of the people in its integrity and its "social guardian" role, which is undermined by the widespread practice of patronage politics.

Concluding remarks

Broadly speaking, no society to start with is intrinsically more corrupt or more lacking in moral standards than another; it is a process shaped by political, social and economic institutions through which the behavioural norms and moral codes evolve and get perpetuated. Understanding those processes may sometimes provide better insights into the performance of an economy than those gained from the mechanistic approach of the Bretton Woods institutions in defining certain governance indicators and analysing and estimating the relationships between those indicators and economic growth by using cross-country comparisons. It also needs to be realised that, besides being interlinked with economic growth, morality in economic dealings is itself a highly desirable aspect of socio-economic progress like many other non-market aspects of well-being. While economic progress is most evident in GDP growth, if that progress starts diminishing the moral standards of a society, that society needs to revisit its values.

Notes

1 Cf. The obituary article on Douglas North by Robert D. Hershey Jr., "Douglas North, a maverick economist, dies at 95", *The New York Times* (Nov. 24, 2015).
2 This particular application of the "Prisoner's Dilemma" problem is akin to the one originally discussed by Amartya Sen and later cited in Basu, Kaushik. 1997, pp. 11–2.
3 For a discussion on such issues, see, for example, Hareford (2005), pp. 181–5.
4 GNI is estimated by adding to GDP the net income received from abroad such as income from foreign assets, but more importantly for many less developed countries, remittances received from the nationals working overseas.
5 *New York Times*, September 29, 1991, p. E1; cited in McMillan (2002), p. 223.

References

Akerlof, G. (1970). "The markets for lemons: Qualitative uncertainty and the market mechanism". *Quarterly Journal of Economics*, vol. 84, pp. 488–500.
Arrow, K. J. (1978). "A cautious case for socialism", Lecture delivered at the Third Lionel Trilling Seminar, April 3, 1978 at Columbia University; reproduced in *Dissent* magazine, Fall 1978.
Arrow, K. J. and Hahn, F. H. (1971). *General Equilibrium Analysis*. San Francisco: Holden-Day.
Axelrod, Robert and Dion, Douglas. (1988). "The further evolution of prevalence of cooperation". *Science*, vol. 242, no. 4884.
Basu, Kaushik. (1997). *Analytical Development Economics: The Less Developed Economy Revisited*. Cambridge, MA: The MIT Press.
Hareford, T. (2005). *The Undercover Economist*. New York: Random House.
Kahneman, Daniel. (2011). *Thinking, Fast and Slow*. UK: Penguin Random House.
Kay, J. (2004). *Culture and Prosperity: Why Some Nations Are Rich but Most Remain Poor*. New York: Harper Collins.

Khan, A. R. (1979). "The Comilla model and the integrated rural development programme of Bangladesh: An experiment in cooperative capitalism". *World Development*, vol. 7, no. 4–5, pp. 397–422.

Mahmud, W. (2002). "National budgets, social spending and public choice: The case of Bangladesh". IDS Working Paper no. 162. Brighton, England: Institute of Development Studies at the University of Sussex.

Mahmud, W. and Osmani, Siddiq. (2017). *The Theory and Practice of Microcredit.* UK: Routledge.

McMillan, John. (2002). *Reinventing the Bazaar, A Natural History of Markets.* New York: W. W. Norton & Company.

North, C. Douglas. (1990). *Institutions, Institutional Changes and Economic Performance.* Cambridge, UK: Cambridge University Press.

5   Amartya Sen's ideas and the Bangladesh story

Introduction

The writings of Amartya Sen, the Indian Nobel laureate economist of Bangladeshi origin, are spread over vast areas of economics, often encroaching other academic disciplines, especially ethics and philosophy. Beyond being an academic of highest distinction, he is also a public intellectual and his overriding concern in both these roles is about how to promote public action and influence public opinion towards achieving an equitable and just society, which particularly addresses the needs of the underprivileged and offers human dignity to all. It is no wonder, therefore, that his ideas are of great relevance for developing countries that are striving to achieve broad-based economic growth and social progress, and this is more so for India and Bangladesh – the two countries that provide the socio-economic settings for much of his empirical works. Sen has praised the remarkable progress in many social development indicators that Bangladesh has achieved compared to India, despite having a much lower per capita income and suffering from the same, or even much worse, institutional and policy failures. By drawing upon Sen's writings on issues ranging from human development and social inequalities to the concepts of freedom and "public reasoning", this chapter aims at understanding the factors underlying Bangladesh's achievements and the challenges that lie ahead. In so doing, the chapter also looks at the applicability of Sen's development ideas in the varying socio-political settings across developing countries.

Making progress in human development

Much of Amartya Sen's work is about widening the definition of economic development beyond mere income growth to include other aspects of human well-being or capabilities. The incorporation of these non-income

DOI: 10.4324/9781003241775-5

aspects of well-being, such as in respect of health and educational outcomes, led him to lay the foundation of the UN Development Programme's (UNDP) *Human Development Index* and to conceptualise poverty and deprivation beyond income-poverty alone. In this respect, he has praised the evidence on Bangladesh's remarkable achievements in various social development indicators, especially since the early 1990s (Dreze and Sen 2013, pp. 58–64). Cross-country comparisons show that in relation to per capita income, Bangladesh has transformed itself during this period from being a laggard to a clear leader in many of the indicators of health, education and demographic outcomes (Mahmud et al. 2013; Asadullah et. al. 2014).[1] The decline achieved in infant and child mortality rates since the early 1990s, for example, is among the fastest in the developing world. Bangladesh has already eliminated gender disparity in primary and secondary school enrolment. Its success in reducing the population growth rate through the adoption of birth control methods is also unique among countries at similar per capita income levels. Within South Asia, Bangladesh has improved its position ahead of India and the region as a whole in a number of these indicators, including average life expectancy at birth, although its per capita income is still significantly below the regional average (Mahmud 2008; Ahluwalia and Mahmud 2004).

Sen has discussed two distinct pathways of making progress in social development indicators: one is "growth-mediated" which works through rapid and broad-based economic growth, thus facilitating better standards of living and generating more public resources for social spending (e.g. South Korea, Singapore); the other is "interventionist" or "support-led" which involves large public social spending on welfare-oriented programmes (e.g., Sri Lanka, Costa Rica, China and the Indian state of Kerala) (Sen 1999, pp. 43–9; Dreze and Sen 1989, pp. 258–9). It is remarkable that Bangladesh's achievements thus far do not exactly fit into either of these typical pathways. While per capita income in Bangladesh has grown at a modestly high and steadily increasing rate since the early 1990s, this alone cannot explain the extent of improvements in the social development indicators as is obvious from the logic of the cross-country comparisons mentioned above. Neither does Bangladesh represent the typical case of "support-led" human development, since cross-country comparisons show that Bangladesh's public spending per capita on both health and education has remained considerably lower than what is expected even at comparable low levels of per capita income (Mahmud et al. 2013; Asadullah et al. 2014). While Bangladesh may have shown a different kind of pathway for achieving rapid progress in social indicators at an initial stage, it will be argued later that Sen's analysis still holds in understanding challenges that lie ahead for continued progress.

Low-cost solutions and social mobilisation

Various hypotheses have been advanced to explain Bangladesh's success in improving social development indicators. Much of it seems to have been due to the adoption of low-cost solutions like the use of oral rehydration saline (ORS) for diarrhoea treatment leading to a decrease in child mortality, and due to increased public awareness created by effective social mobilisation campaigns such as for immunisation or contraceptive use or girls' schooling. Diarrhoea deaths that used to be the single major cause of under-five mortality in Bangladesh have now been greatly reduced by the widespread adoption of the ORS technology, including the use of homemade saline. Again, due to successful social campaigns, Bangladesh has become a leader among developing countries in the rates of child immunisation, which is another factor greatly contributing to the reduction in under-five mortality. For example, the percentage of one-year-olds immunised against measles in Bangladesh had increased to 81 by 2005 compared to 58 in India and 74 for developing countries as a whole.[2] Maternal mortality has been greatly reduced in recent years mainly through easy access to prenatal care, though the rate of medically attended births remains extremely low even by the standards of low-income countries. Underlying these proximate factors, however, there has also been a broader process of social transformation affecting behavioural norms and attitudes such as towards female employment, fertility behaviour and parental incentives for investments in children's health and education (Mahmud 2008). The rapid increase in female labour force participation, including work outside home, has in particular led to positive synergies with fertility behaviour, child health and other social development outcomes. Dreze and Sen (2013, pp. 58–64) particularly emphasise the agency of women in bringing about this social transformation. As to why Bangladesh could benefit from the role of non-government organisations (NGOs) and the female agency in the way other countries could not remains to be better understood, as observed by Amartya Sen.[3]

The scaling up of programmes through the spread of new ideas is helped in Bangladesh by a strong presence of NGOs and also by the density of settlements and their lack of remoteness made possible by an extensive network of rural roads. Since the early 1990s, the government has emphasised developing extensive networks of rural roads.[4] Besides promoting rural development generally, such dense transport links have helped in making services more accessible to the rural communities, especially to women, and in scaling up social development campaigns as mentioned above. Some innovative government initiatives, such as the so-called "food for education" programme, has helped to bring children from poor rural households to the formal school system since the early 1990s, while female school enrolment has been promoted by the introduction of a universal stipend programme for female students attending secondary schools.[5] The female stipend programme has been described as the world's vanguard programme of this type having profound impact on parental attitudes and social norms regarding sending adolescent girls to schools.

While the government's commitment and support for welfare-oriented programmes have had undoubtedly an important role to play, that is only part of the story; the other part, however, has to do with the role of the NGOs. Bangladesh may well be the world's leader in using NGOs as vehicles of social development. NGOs are involved both in the delivery of services and in the scaling up of the interventions through social awareness campaigns.[6] For example, the initial spread of the use of oral saline for diarrhoea treatment, following its discovery at the ICDDR'B in Dhaka, was largely due to the work of BRAC, the largest development NGO in Bangladesh (World Bank 2007; Zohir 2004). The rapid expansion of microcredit programmes may also have been a contributing factor by promoting social interactions and mobility for rural women. Besides the economic impact of microcredit on poverty, the mobilisation of women's credit groups may have led to non-economic gains through enhanced female agency, empowerment and mutual support, thus creating the social environment for other development interventions to work better (Mahmud 2002a; Mahmud and Osmani 2016).

It can be seen that some elements of both "growth-mediated" and "support-led" mechanisms of human development have been at work, since there has been accelerated growth in per capita income and concomitant reduction in poverty since the early 1990s, and some effective government intervention programmes also had a role. What distinguishes Bangladesh's experience from these typical pathways of human development is the demonstrated evidence that much can be achieved even with low public social spending, poor service delivery and still prevalent widespread poverty by effective social campaigns and adoption of low-cost solutions. However, as the gains from low-cost solutions are reaped, continued progress may increasingly depend on higher public social spending and an improvement in service delivery systems. Further reductions in child mortality, for example, will require more expensive child survival interventions, such as hospital-based care to avert neonatal mortality resulting from birth-related complications. Similarly, lowering the currently high, though declining, maternal mortality rate will also require the provision of relatively costly health services. Again, the existing poor quality of schooling may make it difficult to sustain the gains in school enrolment, and there are signs of that already happening, such as reflected in the high rates of school drop-outs as indicated in the official education statistics. In fact, the data from the recent rounds of the Demographic and Health Survey (the survey which provides data for cross-country comparisons by international bodies) reveal an alarming picture of the overall stagnation, or even decline, across a range of the social development indicators since the mid-2010s.

It may also be noted that the progress in social development indicators has been achieved to a large extent by bypassing the widespread problem of poor governance afflicting service delivery. This has been possible by keeping the government campaigns, such as for immunisation or "social" marketing of contraceptives, outside the established structure of service delivery and also by involving the NGOs. But further progress through this route may prove increasingly difficult. Service delivery systems are highly centralised with very few mechanisms for accountability through community participation. The rural healthcare system, for example, is plagued by poor utilisation of services and widespread absenteeism of doctors. In these respects, Bangladesh is no different, and may be worse than India. As Dreze and Sen (2013, p. xi) observe, "the general state of public services in India remains absolutely dismal, and the country's health and education systems in particular have been severely messed up". Moreover, they observe that this is a reflection of larger issues of accountability beyond the cases of health and education, which is even more true for Bangladesh. Clearly, to consolidate the gains made thus far and make further improvements, the challenge lies not only in allocating more budgetary resources for public social spending but also in improving the governance structure of service delivery.

Social inequalities, deprivation and public action

Much of Amartya Sen's concerns are not just about the progress in the social development indicators for the average population of a country, but about inequalities in these indicators and what happens to its deprived sections. In this respect, again, Bangladesh's record so far has not been much disappointing, if at all, which is explained by the very factors that have contributed to this progress; but future challenges will be seen to be more akin to Sen's concerns.

The NGO-based interventions as well as some government programmes like domiciliary contraceptive services have largely targeted households or individuals, mostly poor women, instead of using what Dreze and Sen (1995, pp. 190–1) call "the agency of the public", such as by involving local government institutions. As such, the interventions are mostly effective in promoting self-interested behaviour for increasing individual household welfare, even if the benefits accruing to the targeted households have elements of "public good" (e.g., immunisation, birth control and sanitation). In the absence of effective local government, the NGOs in Bangladesh work almost in parallel with the centralised public service delivery systems; they have not been very successful in working as community-based organisations so as to enable the poor to claim public services or to sanction service failures (Kabeer et al. 2012). This limitation of the NGOs has also meant that they have been less effective in promoting social capital of the kind that contributes to improving social norms and behaviour. This explains the apparent paradox that in spite of the improvements in social development indicators achieved mostly by using the female agency (Dreze and Sen 1995, pp. 58–64), Bangladesh performs poorly in such aspects of female welfare as the incidence of child marriage and repression and violence on women.

In this respect, Bangladesh's experience contrasts with Sen's discussion of how Kerala had early success in social and human development, which was achieved through effective local governance and local-level political mobilisation (Sen 2009, p. 350; Dreze and Sen 1995, pp. 58–64). It is true that some societal characteristics were helpful in the case of Bangladesh as well. For example, relatively low social barriers of class, caste or ethnicity compared to many other developing countries including India, along with opening up of certain economic opportunities, has helped in creating aspirations among the poor for upward economic mobility. These opportunities were provided by the very rapid spread of microcredit enabling rural agricultural families to diversify their sources of income into non-farm activities, the increasing phenomenon of labour migration for temporary overseas employment and the rapid expansion of the export-oriented ready-made garment industry providing employment mostly to young women from poor families; the latter may partly explain why even the poor families are increasingly sending their children to school. However, these aspects of socio-economic mobility of the poor are very different from the political and social mobilisation in Kerala as described by Dreze and Sen.

Admittedly, further progress in many of the social development indicators in Bangladesh could be achieved through the "income-mediated" path, as the living standards improve with the continued increase in per capita income. But without an increase in the current low levels of public social spending, the gains would come mostly from out-of-pocket expenditure and would therefore likely be unequally distributed. This is because family spending on health, education and quality food needed for improved nutrition are found to be income-elastic leading to increasing inequality in such spending among income classes with the increase in average income (Mahmud 2002b). As Dreze and Sen (1989, p. 258) observe, even in the case of "growth-mediated" path of enhancing human development, the role of well-planned public support, especially for basic health and education cannot be denied (as they contrast the experience of, say, South Korea with what they call the "unaimed opulence" of Brazil).

The risks of such increasing inequality in the distribution of the health and educational outcomes are already evident from the past trends in the indicators for those outcomes for which out-of-pocket spending of households matters. Although we have seen that during the past decades of rapid progress the poor may have in fact gained more than the non-poor in school enrolment and infant and child mortality, the reverse seems to have happened in some other indicators, most importantly in child malnutrition (Osmani 2017). This should not, however, be taken to diminish the value of the overall rapid improvement in child malnutrition achieved thus far, in which the poor also have benefited albeit less so than the non-poor. In fact, a recent cross-country study by Headey (2013) has concluded that in the recent decades Bangladesh had recorded one of the fastest prolonged reductions in child underweight and stunting in recorded history, narrowly behind the more celebrated case of Thailand in the 1980s and ahead of several success stories identified in the nutrition literature, such as in Brazil, Mexico and Honduras.

Famine and food security

One important part of Sen's ideas about extreme deprivation of the underprivileged has to do with the analysis of food deprivation and famine. He has extensively analysed the Great Bengal Famine of 1942–44 as well as the 1974 famine in Bangladesh, the epicentre of both of which was the present Rangpur region in north-west Bangladesh (Sen 1977, 1981, 2009, p. 342). Sen's analysis of famines has led him to two well-known propositions: (a) food deprivation of an epochal proportion such as famine does not happen in a *well-functioning* democracy (Indian famines in the British colonial period and the Chinese famine during 1958–61 being the examples of famines occurring allegedly because of lack of democracy) although such a democracy may suffer from chronic food deprivation (e.g., India), and (b) famine happens not necessarily because of shortage in food supply but because of the loss of "food entitlements" of the poor. Further academic debates and analyses have focused on the aspects of democracy that are conducive to preventing famines, such as the scope of public discussion and media coverage, and also the factors that lead to loss of food entitlement of the poor during food crises.

Sen's analyses of famine and food deprivation largely conform to the experience of Bangladesh where ensuring food security has always been a key element in the government's approach to social protection. Although Bangladesh has been far from a fully functioning democracy, there has not been any major episode of food crises since the famine of 1974–75; the underlying reasons for that famine have been analysed by Sen himself and other researchers. Since then, food security has been always a sensitive issue in media coverage and civic activism. It has also been argued that the experience of the famine in the early years of independence in 1974–75 resulted in a public psyche of "never again", thus creating an urgency for the government to ensure food security and the provision of minimum living standards for the poor (Hossain 2017). Government policies towards boosting food production, stabilising food prices and providing safety nets for the poor have all contributed to promoting food security.

An example of the sensitivity towards food security is provided by the recent initiatives in tackling seasonal hunger in an economically depressed region in north-east Bangladesh: the greater Rangpur region. Rangpur is well-known in famine literature; it was among the worst-hit districts in the Great Bengal Famine of 1942–44 and was literally the epicentre of the 1974 famine in Bangladesh (Sen 1977). The region has not only lagged in poverty reduction behind other regions but has also remained particularly vulnerable to seasonal hunger (locally known as *monga*) linked to agricultural crop cycles. Only since the 2000s, the phenomenon has received special attention in the government's poverty reduction and food security programmes. The various recent initiatives undertaken for combating *monga* in Rangpur include the introduction of new crop technology, provision of public works and other safety nets, facilitation of out-migration, asset transfers to the poor and introduction of specially designed microcredit programmes in addition to the regular ones. As a result of these initiatives, the most acute forms of food deprivation characterising *monga*, such as foregoing meals altogether on some days, have now been almost eliminated (Mahmud and Khandker 2012, pp. 186–90).

The initiatives in combating *monga* in Rangpur have been prompted by widespread public awareness, which in turn has been largely created by media reports and civic activism. The resulting public action against *monga* is a testimony that political incentives even in a not-so-well-functioning democracy can be created for combating the severe incidence of seasonal hunger as well, once the phenomenon catches public attention. However, lack of similar awareness may have resulted in neglect of other regions in Bangladesh that are vulnerable to seasonal distress (Mahmud and Khandker 2012, pp. 189–90).

Again, in 2008, Bangladesh faced a potentially severe food crisis in terms of large grain import bills and a severe price hike in the domestic grain markets. The military-backed caretaker government of the time responded by strengthening the food-based social protection programmes including large-scale open market sales of essential foods at subsidised prices in urban areas. The market supply of food grains was augmented through off-takes from government stocks and by importing large quantities of grains – both in the public sector and through private commercial channels. As a result, the per capita availability of food grains actually increased during the food crisis years of 2007 and 2008, even though the prices of both wheat and rice nearly doubled during this time, keeping pace with prices in the international markets. There was no decline in the real wages of day labourers in agriculture and other informal sectors in spite of this sharp price spike (Mahmud and Khandker 2012, p. 44). Although there were predictions that poverty rates would have been adversely affected by the food price increases, not much evidence of that could be found in the subsequent poverty estimates, with the poverty headcount rates falling more rapidly than ever between 2005 and 2010 (from 44 percent to 35 percent). This episode thus provides an interpretation of Sen's idea of food entitlement in a particular context, namely, how a failure of such entitlement of the poor can be prevented even at the time of a severe food price hike if real wages can be kept from falling and various safety net measures are put in place.

Democracy, institutional development and economic progress

In the recent book co-authored by Jean Dreze and Amartya Sen, titled *An Uncertain Glory: India and Its Contradictions*, they make the strong assertion that "the history of world development offers few other examples, if any, of an economy growing so fast for so long with such limited results in terms of reducing human deprivations" (Dreze and Sen 2013, p. ix). They contrast this performance with Bangladesh's "astonishing achievements" in certain aspects of social progress as discussed earlier in this chapter (although they hasten to add that Bangladesh remains one of the most deprivation-ridden countries of the world with the same kinds of policy failures as in India; p. 59). In fact, Bangladesh's contradictions lie elsewhere; its institutional development has thus far lagged far behind its achievements in socio-economic progress. Bangladesh now ranks among the few fastest growing economies in the world while it scores very poorly in most indicators of economic and political governance including the World Bank's "Ease of Doing Business Index" and the World Economic Forum's "Global Competitiveness Index". While a close association between the quality of institutions and economic performance is now widely recognised, the moot question is: How far can Bangladesh sustain progress without commensurate institution-building towards better governance? A related question is: What happens to economic performance as the formal structure of "multi-party electoral democracy" shows signs of regress, as has been happening in many new democracies including Bangladesh (e.g., the so-called mixed or hybrid democracies).

The answer to these questions can be sought only indirectly from Amartya Sen's writings on related topics. He is primarily concerned with how to make the already established democratic institutions, such as in India, more responsive to the demands for social justice. He also discusses how institutional and human capabilities interact with economic growth in high-performing economies that already have fairly strong formal institutions of governance, albeit of very different kinds such as shown by the contrast between India and China (Dreze and Sen 2013; Sen 1999). At the risk of being too simplistic, one could summarise his views as follows.

Before China introduced market-oriented reforms in the late 1970s, it had already in place economic and social conditions that were conducive to respond to such reforms towards broad-based economic expansion, such as land reform, near-universal basic education, provision of basic public health, high female participation in the labour force and a functioning system of local governance. The existence of the same pre-reform conditions may explain the success of other East Asian "miracle economies" (e.g., South Korea, Taiwan, Singapore and also Japan in the earlier period) in achieving broad-based economic growth by adopting market-oriented policies. Sen laments that India was nowhere near achieving these solid foundations of broad-based economic expansion (Dreze and Sen 1995, p. 197).

However, India had a well-established democratic institutional structure at the time of the introduction of market reforms in the late 1980s and early 1990s, and its success in accelerating economic growth in the post-reform era helped to dispel an earlier notion that democracy may not be conducive to, or even can be a hindrance for high economic growth (Dreze and Sen 2009, pp. 345–8). Sen believes that the Indian democracy is seriously compromised by high inequality and the lack of voice of the disadvantaged, and that democracy does not stand for electoral politics or civil liberties alone. But even in its compromised state, Indian democracy in his opinion offers enough scope for popular movements, agitation and public discourses to flourish and resist the neglect of interests of the underprivileged. This explains his passionate advocacy for exploiting the democratic space for "public reasoning" in the form of argumentation, discourses and agitation towards achieving a more just society (Dreze and Sen 2013, p. xii).

Amartya Sen clearly prefers the democratic, rather than the authoritarian way of achieving economic development for several reasons. Civil liberties and democratic rights are desirable goals by themselves as "constituent components" of development, irrespective of the extent to which these are also conducive to economic development. There is also no evidence, supported by serious studies, that democracy is inimical to economic growth, so that there should not be a split in the choice of whether one wants development instead of democracy. Economic development is not for making a country fit for democracy but to be achieved through democracy, as Sen argues. As long as the economies are booming and the economic fortunes of all classes go up, democratic rights may not be that important; but at the time of any economic crises, the political and economic rights may be desperately missed by those whose livelihoods are severely affected, which in turn may lead to disruptive regime changes. Sen thus argues that the potential capacity of democracy in providing economic security to the vulnerable population may in fact be more extensive than famine prevention (e.g., his thesis of why famine does not occur in a functioning democracy). All these observations have profound implications for the so-called "hybrid democracies" regarding the directions in which they should try to achieve social and economic development.

Beyond Amartya Sen's writings, there is, of course, a large amount of academic literature seeking to explain the economic success of the East Asian economies; there is also a growing number of more recent studies about how the new democracies (created from the so-called third wave of democratisation) flourish or decay and how the nature of ruling regimes – democratic, authoritarian or a mix of the two – affect the quality of economic performance. It is now well accepted that developing countries can achieve high economic performance both under democracy – as in India – and under authoritarian regimes, as in contemporary China and the erstwhile East Asian countries. The common element shared between these contrasting regimes is a system of "accountability" at all tiers of governance, which lies behind the more proximate preconditions for good economic management such as efficiency and the primacy of public good over private gains through rent-seeking. As distinct from accountability, Sen would also like to add the notion of "responsibility" in the discharge of duty, say, by a public official; while the former can be ensured through administrative mechanisms, the latter is largely a matter of individual morality.[7]

Accountability mechanisms in the governance system

The way accountability in the governance system is ensured in a well-functioning democracy is too well-known to need elaboration, but the issue is more complex in the case of successful authoritarian regimes. In the case of the erstwhile authoritarian regimes in East Asia, the key to ensuring accountability lay in their quality of economic bureaucracies which were "technically insulated" from patronage politics and whose policies were subject to performance-based scrutiny. In China, the governance reforms introduced in the wake of economic liberalisation have put in place a hierarchical system of strict accountability within the communist party's bureaucracy regarding achieving economic targets. As one commentator on China has aptly brought out the contrast in the structure of performance incentives under democratic and authoritarian regimes: in democracy, politics is interesting while bureaucracy is boring; in China, the reverse is true.

The new breed of authoritarian democracies may try to deliberately pursue an approach of "technical insulation" of economic policymaking, as Malaysia did under Mahathir's previous regime, but these regimes generally lack the kind of governance effectiveness or party cohesion that is needed for mimicking the purely authoritarian mechanisms of accountability. At the same time, the regimes have the advantage of having some of the democratic accountability mechanisms even with poorly functioning democratic institutions. So long as the ruling regimes face periodic well-participated elections, they are aware of the risk that even flawed or rigged elections may be lost; this may happen if the extent of corruption in high places and the excesses of patronage politics cross certain thresholds of public tolerance. The voice of the opposition party even in a weakly functioning parliament of elected representatives may sensitise public opinion against excesses committed by the ruling regime. In case of rigged elections and non-functional parliaments, the watchdog bodies and the judiciary can act as a fall back, even when the integrity of these state institutions is compromised to an extent. Beyond these institutional mechanisms of accountability, the media and civic activism can be another fall back. Such a regime also knows that its survival ultimately lies in its legitimacy in the eye of the common people, unless it increasingly resorts to coercive measures to stay in power. In a hybrid regime, that legitimacy can be maintained only by compensating the democratic deficits by delivering visible rapid economic progress.

Herein lies a potential for both a virtuous and a vicious cycle in the new hybrid authoritarian democracies. Strengthening the democratic institutions of accountability may contribute to creating an environment for better economic performance that may in turn enhance the legitimacy of the regime, thus creating incentives for the regime to further loosen its authoritarian grip on those institutions. The opposite is a downward spiral of lesser accountability leading to poorer economic performance and even further curtailing of the democratic accountability mechanisms in the face of declining regime legitimacy. Only countries with exceptionally strong growth drivers may escape such a vicious cycle, at least for some time.

How is Bangladesh currently situated in this governance-development nexus? As already indicated, economic and social progress in Bangladesh has had to contend with a serious problem of governance dysfunction. One hypothesis is that the progress so far has not been the result of a coordinated overall development strategy pursued by an efficient and accountable governance system; instead, the confluence of various factors and the leading roles of different actors at different times have resulted in often unanticipated outcomes (Khan 2015). Examples include the donor-supported family planning campaigns in the 1980s; the NGOs that emerged in the post-independence period primarily as relief agencies but later transformed into major developmental agents for service delivery including the provision of microfinance; the combination of various factors that made it possible for the export-oriented garment industry to make a foothold in the country and later becoming a major player in the global market; the opening up of the market in the Middle East for the export of unskilled or semi-skilled labour; the pioneering role of certain government agencies such as the Local Government Engineering Department (LGED) that went even beyond its mandate in constructing extensive rural road networks; and so on.

Such development does not just happen without an active role and support of the government. How does one then reconcile such a role of the government amid widespread governance dysfunction? Although there was a transition from an authoritarian rule to parliamentary democracy in 1991, the political culture is one that does not allow democratic practices to flourish, or one that can hardly deliver an accountable and transparent state. The core governance system is characterised by a dysfunctional parliament, highly confrontational politics, the absence of democratic practice within the major parties, politicisation of the state institutions, a corrupt and inefficient bureaucracy and a widespread culture of patronage politics in which spoils and privileges are parcelled out to different clientele groups as an essential tool of political management (Mahmud and Mahmud 2014).

Yet, despite such governance dysfunction, the state appears to deliver on many of the welfare promises, as already discussed. One explanation may lie in the fact that not all political incentives have been inimical to achieving the welfare goals. The national elections held under the system of caretaker government since the transition to parliamentary democracy in the early 1990s were seen as fair and credible. People seemed to have demonstrated a willingness to move against regimes once they crossed some vaguely defined threshold with respect to poor governance and corruption, as evidenced by the fall of the successive governments led by the Awami League and the Bangladesh Nationalist Party (BNP). This created an incentive structure in which public representatives tried to respond to the genuine popular sentiments to win re-election while still engaging in rent-seeking activities (Mahmud and Mahmud 2014; Mahmud et al. 2008). In some instances, the support for public social spending was seen as a political win–win because the members of parliament could take credit for the expansion of welfare programmes in their constituencies; this was good for their voter base in spite of the leakage of resources, and such spending also provided rent-seeking opportunities for their clients. However, the system of the caretaker government has now been abolished by the current government of the Awami League, which since then has consolidated its grip on power and emerged as the single dominant party. The governance system now looks more like that of the so-called hybrid or mixed democracy, so that one needs to reassess the country's prospects for continued progress in the context of such a regime.

Another hypothesis is that the absence of formal accountability mechanisms, such as a functioning parliament or strong state institutions like the higher judiciary, has been compensated by certain non-institutional mechanisms. Activism by the media and the civil society has often proved as a countervailing force, as in the case of public action for mitigating the seasonal hunger in north-west Bangladesh, as discussed earlier. The reason why successive regimes in Bangladesh, democratic or otherwise, have felt the need for portraying for themselves a developmental public welfare stance may have even a deeper root. Such a stance is needed for the legitimacy of a ruling regime in the eye of the general public, given the strong economic aspirations of the people that can be traced back to the struggle for independence. The question, however, arises about whether the legitimacy-seeking mechanism of accountability mentioned above could alone provide enough countervailing force against the governance problems that may constrain further economic and social progress. Although the governance environment has been barely adequate so far to cope with an economy breaking out of stagnation and extreme poverty, it may increasingly prove a barrier to putting the economy firmly on a path of modernisation, global integration and poverty reduction (Mahmud 2007).

Social choice and public reasoning

With Bangladesh looking increasingly like a one-party-dominated hybrid democracy, the question arises about how to avoid the vicious cycle of further erosion of democratic accountability mechanisms discussed earlier, and, instead, move towards a governance system offering more political and civil liberties. Amartya Sen's passionate advocacy of what he calls "public reasoning" is relevant in this context (Sen 1999, 2009). The idea is to generate public opinion and influence social attitudes regarding important social and political issues through enlightened debates, discussions and agitation, given the space offered by the prevailing governance system for such activities.

The idea of "public reasoning" comes from his firm conviction about the value of reasoned argumentation in resolving contested issues, for which the Indian society (including, of course, the Bengalis) has a long historical tradition, as elaborately discussed in his book, *The Argumentative Indian* (Sen 2005). The idea is also based on the practical extensions he made to the so-called theory of "social choice" that looks at the possibility of deriving preference orderings of the society in a democratic way (e.g., by majority votes). Kenneth Arrow, one of the earliest Nobel laureates in economics (1972), formulated this theory by showing that the democratic rule of majority votes can provide thoroughly inconsistent or illogical preference orderings among, say, some alternative social outcomes.[8] The subsequent academic discussions around this theory by Sen and other economists had a constructive impact on the theory showing that there can be other approaches to democratically derive preferences for the good of the society at least for a limited range of choices. An individual, instead of acting like what Sen calls a self-centred "social moron", has multi-dimensional preferences which reflect his ethical values and commitment to his community and society at large (Sen 1997, pp. 99, 102–6; Sen 2009, pp. 87–103, 279–82). Hence the need for what Sen calls "public reasoning", that is, informed debates and argumentation to sway public opinion in support for such causes as promoting female empowerment or protecting minority rights or various other measures towards establishing a just society. Such "public reasoning" is needed all the more, as Sen argues, on the ground that even consistent preference orderings obtained by majority votes may violate certain minimum ethical standards, such as not protecting the rights of the minorities in a society (Sen 1997). Of course, there will be a diversity of perspectives and priorities of individuals or groups of individuals which may not be all amenable to reconciliation, but that should not diminish the value of "public reasoning".

In the context of contemporary Bangladesh, the questions may arise as to how much space is there to demand political rights (e.g., electoral democracy) and whether the curtailment of political rights will allow demands for social rights (e.g., civil liberties, women empowerment, rights of the disadvantaged, environmental protection and reducing public health hazards from pollution). Much will depend on the freedom of media and space for civic activism, both of which are passionately advocated by Amartya Sen. Hamilton (2020), for example, while being generally appreciative of Sen's advocacy for "public reasoning", points out the loose ends in Sen's thinking when it comes to a repressive regime that allows little space for political dissent.[9] The ruling regime itself may benefit from public opinion in support of many reforms that are related to sustaining the economic growth momentum but are resisted by vested interests, such as reforms addressing the share market scams or wilful defaults of bank loans that are now beginning to shake the confidence of depositors in the financial institutions, or money laundering resulting in large-scale capital flight, or unlawful grabbing of land including riverbanks, hills and forests that is seriously depleting the already meagre environmental resources. The government may also be more inclined to steer the right course if public discourses can show that, in Bangladesh's socio-cultural setting, economic growth is likely to be helped by the supportive environment of a liberal democratic climate rather than by a fiercely ruthless regime or a regime primarily drawing support from crony capitalism and patronage politics (Sen 2009, p. 348).

Social campaigns may also be effective for addressing many adverse aspects of governance where the extent of legal and regulatory enforcement mechanisms interact with the evolution of moral standards: the poor work ethics in government agencies leading to widespread corruption, the culture of large-scale tax evasion, food adulteration or pollution and environmental degradation. Then there are social issues like child marriage or child labour which are more in the domain of social norms and attitudes than that of governance reforms. After all, much of Bangladesh's achievements so far have been due to the ingenuity and entrepreneurship of the common people, often helped by effective social campaigns. Efforts for achieving further progress in many such areas may not wait for political rights of electoral democracy and civil liberties to be fully restored. At least that much lesson may be learnt by rereading and reinterpreting Amartya Sen's writings in the context of contemporary Bangladesh.

Notes

1 This can be seen from the regression results in Mahmud et al. (2013) and Asadullah et al. (2014) which show for different time periods the extent of deviations of the actual values of these indicators from what are expected at the level of per capita income of Bangladesh.
2 See UNDP (2007), pp. 248–50.
3 Comments made by Amartya Sen on the author's keynote presentation at the opening session of a year-long study programme on Sen's works organised by *Banglar Pathshala*, Dhaka, March 9, 2020.
4 The road density in Bangladesh, as measured by road length per unit of area, is approximately the same as that in the UK and is higher than in many other OECD countries; World Bank (2005), p. 37.
5 Under the "food for education" programme, children from poor rural families were given wheat rations (later monetised) for regular school attendance.
6 For a comprehensive account of the NGO sector in Bangladesh, see World Bank (2007).
7 Amartya Sen made this comment on the author's keynote presentation at a seminar in Dhaka held on March 9, 2020, as mentioned in an earlier note.
8 Consider, for example, among three choices, A may be preferred to B by a majority (say, two individuals out of a total three), B may be preferred to C

again by a majority, but C is preferred to A by a majority as well, which will not thus yield a consistent social preference ordering among the three choices.
9 See Foreword by Jean Dreze in Hamilton (2020), p. xii.

References

Ahluwalia, I. J. and Mahmud, W. (2004). "Economic transformation and social development in Bangladesh". *Economic and Political Weekly*, vol. 39, no. 36, pp. 4009–11.

Asadullah, M. N., Savoia A. and Mahmud, W. (2014). "Paths to development: Is there a Bangladesh surprise?" *World Development*, vol. 62, pp. 138–54.

Dreze, J. and Sen, Amartya K. (1989). *Hunger and Public Action*. New Delhi: Oxford University Press.

Dreze, J. and Sen, Amartya. (1995). *India: Economic Development and Social Opportunity*. New Delhi: Oxford University Press.

Dreze, J. and Sen, Amartya. (2013). *An Uncertain Glory: India and Its Contradictions*. London, UK: Allen Lane.

Hamilton, L. (2020). *How to Read Amartya Sen*. Gurgaon: Penguin Random House India.

Headey, D. (2013). "Developmental drivers of nutritional change: A cross-country analysis". *World Development*, vol. 42, pp. 76–88.

Hossain, N. (2017). *The Aid Lab: Understanding Bangladesh's Unexpected Success*. Oxford, UK: Oxford University Press.

Kabeer, N., Castro, J. and Mahmud, S. (2012). "NGOs and the political empowerment of poor people in rural Bangladesh: Cultivating the habits of democracy?" *World Development*, vol. 40, no. 10, pp. 2044–62.

Khan, A. R. (2015). *The Economy of Bangladesh: A Quarter Century of Development*. Basingstoke, UK: Palgrave Macmillan.

Mahmud, S. (2002a). "Informal groups in rural Bangladesh: Operation and outcomes". In J. Heyer, F. Stewart and R. Thorpe (eds.), *Group Behaviour and Development*: *Is the Market Destroying Cooperation?* Oxford: Oxford University Press.

Mahmud, W. (2002b). "National budgets, social spending and public choice: The case of Bangladesh". IDS Working Paper no. 162. Brighton, UK: Institute of Development Studies, University of Sussex.

Mahmud, W. (2007). "Bangladesh: Development outcomes in the context of globalization". In Ernesto Zedillo (ed.), *The Future of Globalization: Explorations in Light of Recent Turbulence*. Abingdon, UK: Routledge.

Mahmud, W. (2008). "Social development: Pathways, surprises and challenges". *Indian Journal of Human Development*, vol. 2, no. 1, pp. 79–92.

Mahmud, W., Ahmed, S. and Mahajan, S. (2008). "Economic reforms, growth and governance: The political economy aspects of Bangladesh's development surprise". In D. Brady and M. Spence (eds.), *Leadership and Growth*, Chapter 8, pp. 227–54. Washington, DC: World Bank on behalf of the Commission on Growth and Development.

Mahmud, W. and Khandker, S. (2012). *Seasonal Hunger and Public Policies: Evidence from Northwest Bangladesh*. Washington DC: World Bank Publications.

Mahmud, W., Asadullah, M. N. and Savoia, A. (2013). "Bangladesh's achievements in social development indicators: Explaining the puzzle". *Economic and Political Weekly*, vol. 48, no. 44, pp. 26–8.

Mahmud, W. and Mahmud, S. (2014). "Development, welfare and governance: Explaining Bangladesh's 'development surprise'". In G. Koehler and D. Chopra (eds.), *Development and Welfare Policy in South Asia*. Abingdon, UK: Routledge.

Mahmud, W. and Osmani, S. R. (2016). *The Theory and Practice of Microcredit*. Abingdon, UK: Routledge.

Osmani, S. R. (2017). "Eradicating poverty and minimizing inequality for ensuring shared prosperity in Bangladesh. A background paper for the Perspective Plan (2021–2041)". General Economics Division, Planning Commission, Government of Bangladesh, Dhaka, December.

Sen, Amartya K. (1977). "Starvation and exchange entitlements: A general approach and its application to the Great Bengal Famine". *Cambridge Journal of Economics*, vol. 1, no. 1, pp. 33–59.

Sen, Amartya K. (1981). *Poverty and Famines: An Essay on Entitlement and Deprivation*. New York and Oxford, UK: Oxford University Press.

Sen, Amartya K. (1999). *Development as Freedom*. Oxford, UK: Oxford University Press.

Sen, Amartya K. (2005). *The Argumentative Indian: Writings on Indian Culture, History and Identity*. London: Penguin Books.

Sen, Amartya K. (2009). *The Idea of Justice*. London: Allen Lane.

World Bank. (2005). *Attaining the Millennium Goals in Bangladesh*. Washington, DC: World Bank (South Asia Region).

World Bank. (2007). *Economics and Governance of Nongovernmental Organizations in Bangladesh*. Dhaka, Bangladesh: University Press Limited, published for the World Bank, Dhaka.

UNDP. (2007). *Human Development Report 2007/2008*. New York and Oxford: Oxford University Press, for the United Nations Development Programme.

Zohir, S. (2004). "NGO sector in Bangladesh: An overview". *Economic and Political Weekly*, vol. 39, no. 36, pp. 4109–13.

6 Is there an economics of social business?

Introduction

The idea of socially oriented business is not new, although Nobel Peace laureate Muhammad Yunus has certainly given an enormous impetus to it by his articulate branding of it as "social business". The reason his campaign has caught so much public attention is at least partly to do with its timing. Global capitalism, driven by the singular pursuit of profit, has in recent times exposed some of the worst brutalities of the system – repeated global financial meltdown, the increasing concentration of wealth and the unmitigated environmental damage associated with the looming threat of climate change. French economist Thomas Piketty's (2014) convincing analysis in his recent bestselling book *Capital in the Twenty-First Century* as to why the current capitalist system will lead to an unabated process of wealth concentration has only helped to add fuel to the fire of public discontent. It is not surprising that the global business community has shown considerable interest in the idea of social business, at least in its public posture, almost as a penance for the sins that have been committed.

While many top business schools worldwide have already included the topic of social business in their curricula, the response from the mainstream economists is at best lukewarm. There could be two reasons for this apathy. First, the idea of social business may appear to be too fuzzy for the analytical tools of economics – an academic discipline that claims the status of science. Muhammad Yunus describes it as a viable business model which has a social mission rather than profit-seeking as its main purpose and the owners of which do not earn any dividend from the profit (Yunus 2007). That definition in fact fits a range of socially oriented business models, all of which may not strictly qualify as social business according to the criteria set by Yunus and Weber (2010, pp. 1–9). There are clearly some borderline cases as we shall discuss later. Second, while admitting that many market distortions do exist, economists are accustomed to the elegant theorising

DOI: 10.4324/9781003241775-6

of the efficiency of the market economy that is rooted in the premise of self-seeking behaviour and the "profit motive". This academic tradition has continued ever since Adam Smith famously remarked that we owed our breakfast not to the benevolence of the baker or the butcher but to their self-interest.

The main purpose of this chapter is to explore if and how the idea of social business could be reconciled with mainstream economic thinking. In doing so, however, we pay relatively less attention to the extent to which social businesses can actually succeed in achieving their professed social goals in practice. Even less attention is paid to the promise of social business in bringing about any significant change in the way global capitalism works. After all, we are only looking at some analytical aspects of the concept, while, in Yunus' own words, the full promise of the concept of social business lies in the realm of "dreams" that cannot be perceived or realised "by using the analytical minds trained to deal with hard information that is currently available" (Yunus and Weber 2010, p. 206).

Can social business be uniquely defined?

The defining characteristics of a social business, according to its proponents, are that (a) its profit stays with it and is not paid back as dividend; (b) instead of maximising profits, its mission is to do some social good (such as in the field of education, public health, access to technology and environment protection); and (c) it must be able to attain financial sustainability (Yunus and Weber 2010, p. 3). These characteristics should distinguish a social business from a company doing corporate philanthropy, that is, setting aside some of its profits for spending on what are known as corporate social responsibility (CSR) activities. No matter how much profit is set aside for philanthropy, there needs to be something in the way the business itself is run (that is, having some social motive) other than merely generating profits. The problem, however, is to clearly define that "social" element as a yardstick against which a social business can be clearly identified.

However, even corporate philanthropy in the form of CSR may be part of a business model. Modern-day smart company executives worldwide know that strategic spending on CSR activities can be in the long-run business interest of their firms. Thus, CSR is sometimes seen as a way of delivering some social good, such as promoting healthy foods, with the objective of cashing on the goodwill thus created for the company in the long run. There is increasing interest in the global business community in what is called "impact investments", that is, investments made by companies and other organisations with the intention to generate social and environmental impact alongside a financial return.

The phenomenon is, however, reversed in the case of a social business, which takes advantage of a viable business model while pursuing its overriding social goals. But since both the models incorporate some social element in the running of the business and differ only in their ultimate goal, the distinction may sometimes get blurred. In fact, a social mission and a commercial motive may coexist at least in the initial stage of many innovative ventures, such as those taking advantage of a new technology. An example in Bangladesh is the mobile-phone-based money transfer system, called *bKash*, which was conceived for facilitating the money transfers of relatively poor people, such as the financial transactions of small traders or urban workers' remittances to their families in rural areas.[1] This e-money model has turned out to be extremely successful and has been adopted by a number of commercial banks in Bangladesh as a profitable business. India's giant dairy business, known by its product brand name *Amul*, provides a uniquely successful model of a cooperative organisation running a big business. It originated from a cooperative of dairy farmers set up many decades ago to protect the farmers from the exploitation of market intermediaries and ensure for them a fair price for their milk; over the years it has grown into an apex cooperative body linking more than 3 million dairy farmers and running a globally famous dairy business (Heredia 1997). There are many such examples of business model worldwide for which it may be difficult to make a clear distinction between socially oriented enterprises developing successful businesses and for-profit businesses having a social mission (Mills-Scofield 2013).

An advantage of social business over conventional corporate philanthropy, as argued by its proponents, is that once an investment is made in a social business, its benefits will continue as long as that business remains in operation, while companies have to allocate funds annually for their CSR activities. This is similar to the advantage that a revolving fund for a microcredit programme may have over annual transfers to the poor under social safety net programmes. It is thus no coincidence that Muhammad Yunus happens to be the pioneer of both microcredit and social business. However, even this characterisation of social business leaves some grey area in the case of companies that are set up with a major (if not the sole) objective of generating profits for doing philanthropy. These companies may be run on a purely commercial basis, but the profits are wholly or largely spent on socially oriented activities, thus providing a sustainable source of funds for spending on such activities. Examples in Bangladesh include some commercial enterprises owned by the *Kumudini Welfare Trust*, the entire profits of which are diverted to spending on the charitable activities of the Trust. Another example is Renata Pharmaceuticals – a purely market-oriented and a reputed company in its field in Bangladesh; a half of its annual profit goes to the *Sajida Foundation*, which is a microfinance institution but also carries out many social welfare activities. It is noteworthy that both Renata Pharmaceuticals and the *Kumudini Welfare Trust* are recipients of an annual CSR award in Bangladesh sponsored by the Standard Chartered Bank; the award committee (which the present author happens to chair) had doubts about whether the conventional idea of CSR, rather than some notion of socially oriented business, applied to these companies.

While the conventional CSR spending of a company, often carried out by setting up a foundation, may lie outside the concept of social business, a company can set up a subsidiary that may very well qualify as a social business. In fact, experiments in setting up this kind of social business involving large multinationals seem to have so far caught the most attention. The "Grameen" family of companies in Bangladesh, which are joint ventures with reputed multinationals, belong to this genre of social business. The joint venture company called Grameen-Danone, for example, is one such experiment aimed at producing low-priced yogurt containing micro-nutrients missing in the ordinary diets of children from poor families while also helping to market milk produced by poor rural households. Among other such companies, Grameen-BASF is to make and market chemically treated mosquito nets at affordable prices for the poorest; Grameen-Veolia is to provide safe drinking water at an affordable price in villages where arsenic contamination of groundwater is a serious problem; Grameen-Adidas is to produce shoes for low-income people, particularly to protect rural children from parasitic diseases transmitted through walking barefoot; and Grameen-Intel is to help solve various problems of the rural poor, for example, by providing healthcare in villages (Yunus 2007; Yunus and Weber 2010). What remains to be seen is whether these companies can attain financial viability while also catering to the needs of the intended beneficiaries (even then, there will be some hidden subsidies from the parent companies, at least in terms of R&D and related overhead costs).

Another kind of social business is represented by "a profit-making company owned by poor people, either directly or through a trust that is dedicated to a predetermined social cause" (Yunus and Weber 2010, p. 2). This leaves out co-operatives that are run purely for profit to benefit their member-shareholders and serve no particular social objective. But, as argued by Yunus (2010, pp. 7–8), co-operatives may be regarded as social business, if they fulfil the double criteria of (a) being owned by poor people, and (b) are run in a way so as to create some social benefits, such as housing co-ops that make an affordable home for the working-class people, or banking co-ops that provide financial services to otherwise underserved clients. An example is the Self-Employed Women's Organization (SEWA) of India, which is a trade union that organises women for self-help by providing financial and other services to its rank-and-file members. Similarly, Grameen Bank, whose majority shareholders are its member-borrowers, may also fit this category of social business (Yunus and Weber 2010, p. 2). However, in both these cases, the ownership of the poor in terms of earning dividends may be only notional, since their clients benefit mainly through the financial services that they provide (e.g., small credit and deposit schemes). In fact, the claim for Grameen Bank to be a social business perhaps lies more in its having become a financially self-sustainable microfinance institution (MFI) rather than in its member-borrowers owning the Bank and earning dividends from its profits.

Whether the MFIs qualify as social business remains another grey area. Other than Grameen Bank, the microfinance programmes in Bangladesh are run by numerous non-government organisations (NGOs) which were initially established for "social mobilisation" of the rural communities along with service delivery, but later on shifted their emphasis to the provision of credit to the poor – hence now commonly known as NGO-MFIs. Thus, while their social mission is not in doubt, the test for qualifying as social business lies in their ability to become financially sustainable.[2] Some of the large ones among them may now very well pass this test; although initially dependent on external funds, the microcredit programmes of these NGO-MFIs have now become financially self-sustainable and have even started generating surplus for funding non-credit services for their clients. In contrast, there is an alternative profit-oriented model of microcredit programmes practised in many countries, especially in South America, with the main goal of maximising shareholder dividend; these MFIs clearly lie outside the scope of social business.

Businesses of NGO-MFIs

Besides their microfinance operations, large NGO-MFIs (stands for non-government organisations doing microfinance) in Bangladesh have gone into commercial ventures that again may lie in the grey area of social business, if one were to go by the strict criteria set for defining such a business. Although these enterprises do not generate any private dividend from profits, they are often run purely as profit-oriented businesses, sometimes even catering to upmarket consumer demand (e.g., fashion clothing). Yet, these commercial enterprises have a potentially important role to play in helping to reinforce the social goals of microcredit programmes for poverty alleviation and employment creation. This they can do by bringing the micro-enterprises of the borrower-clients of the MFIs into their supply chains and supporting their scaling up, such as through the provision of market access and adoption of improved production technology (including product design and quality assurance). The businesses of MGO-MFIs can have a competitive edge over other commercial businesses, since they can economise on overhead costs due to their institutional presence in rural areas and networks with a large pool of spatially dispersed small producers. On the downside, NGO-MFIs often lack business experience and depend initially on low-cost investment funds leading to high rates of failures of such businesses.

There are already some notable examples of many such innovative MFI businesses. One of these, *Aarong*, is operated by BRAC on commercial lines to market domestically and internationally products of small/micro-enterprises (such as handicrafts, garments, handloom and sericulture products and pasteurised milk and milk products). Another example is *Grameen Check*, a handloom product that is marketed both in domestic and international markets. Grameen Telecom, a minority-share partner of a multinational mobile operator, offered a technology to create an income-generating activity for its borrowers – the so-called "phone ladies" providing mobile telephone service for villagers. The BRAC Bank, another venture of BRAC established in 2001, goes beyond traditional commercial banking to serve small entrepreneurs through dedicated countrywide so-called SME (small and medium enterprises) branches. Its small-business banking model emphasises relationship banking and collateral-free lending of up to US$14,000, with wide coverage in rural areas (WB 2012, p. 164). Clearly, the "social" element in the running of a business may come in different shades and may not always be amenable to unambiguous categorisation.

Reconciling with economic theorising

Can the concept of social business be accommodated within the main body of economic theorising? Or, at the least, can the analytical tools of economics be applied to explain and evaluate the working of a social business? Neither the proponents of social business nor academic economists have shown much interest to answer these questions. Apart from the definitional ambiguities, economists may be uncomfortable with the absence of the profit-maximising behaviour which lies at the core of the theory of firm and welfare economics based on the *efficiency* of the market system. As mentioned earlier, the emphasis on the profit motive in economics goes back to Adam Smith who was a great believer of the virtues of the so-called "invisible hand" that is supposed to work through the self-interested behaviour of businessmen. Amartya Sen, for example, has often lamented this singular focus on profit motive; fortunately, he says, the real world is richer in human qualities than described in economics textbooks (Sen 1984).

Alternatives to the profit motive and the self-seeking behaviour of economic agents have occasionally appeared in the analytical constructs of economics, but never became part of the mainstream. According to a long-forgotten strand of economic theorising, the success of a competitive free-enterprise economy can be shown to depend on people pursuing *self-chosen* interest, which can be altruistic or anything else (Winter, Jr. 1969). While these theoretical results are derived under highly restrictive conditions, one may argue that the assumptions underlying the welfare economics of the competitive market economy are themselves far removed from reality and serve only as a point of departure.

There are also economic arguments that point to incentives of economic agents other than self-interest underlying the efficiency of the market system. For example, it was once argued by some economists that the so-called "Japanese ethos" of loyalty of the Japanese workers to their firm and to their co-workers rather than individual self-seeking was the key to the success of the Japanese economy (Morishima 1982). It is noteworthy that the proponents of social business argue that such businesses can provide an enjoyable work environment in which workers have a sense of pursuing a social mission (Yunus and Weber 2010, p. 3). The "Japanese ethos", in contrast to the Western business culture, is in fact an example of a broader phenomenon analysed by Hirsch (1977) regarding how behavioural modification by breaking away from individual self-interest can help better achieve the fulfilment of those very interests. Incorporating motivations other than self-interest in the working of the market economy should not be therefore altogether new to economic theorising.

There may, in fact, be a promising way of reconciling the idea of social business with mainstream economic thinking – at least in the context of the literature on public policy. A social business is expected to achieve its social objectives by producing some socially oriented products or services that are not supplied by profit-oriented businesses. Examples may include marketing products that have public health benefits or promoting some environment-friendly or employment generating technology. These products and services are supposed to have what economists call "public good" characteristics with beneficial externalities, that is, their benefits extend beyond what would be otherwise reflected in the market demand and business profits. As a result, these goods and services will be under-supplied, or not be supplied at all, by profit-maximising businesses. In contrast, when these are produced and supplied by a social business having no profit-maximisation goal, an implicit subsidy is involved; it is only that the subsidies in this case come not from the public exchequer but from the foregone business profits. Such subsidies can be justified in economic theory as a legitimate means of correcting market distortions and deficiencies arising from the so-called economic externalities. The literature on welfare economics is replete with examples of both positive and negative externalities, such as arising from the "public good" nature of certain marketed items and from the adverse environmental effects that do not figure in a firm's production costs. While private firms can be restrained from doing harm to the environment by imposing an environmental tax on them, a social business is supposed to protect the environment on its own. Viewed in this way, social business can be a means of "internalising" the externalities in its business model.

The above line of reasoning can perhaps be a more fruitful way of conceptualising social business instead of attempting to reconstruct the entire logic of the *efficiency* of the profit-oriented market economy. Furthermore, by adopting such an analytical approach, it is possible to show that, far from creating distortions in the market economy, social businesses can in fact be so designed as to address at least two major sources of shortcomings of the market economy: first, the inefficiencies resulting from the so-called "externalities", and second, the fact that the market economy allocates resources "efficiently" only in relation to the market demand resulting from a given distribution of income. Thus, producing and marketing consumer items at affordable prices targeted to the poor can be seen as a way of trying to redress the income distributional problem that is inherent even in an otherwise efficiently functioning market economy. The same is true for social businesses that may be set up for adopting production technologies or for marketing products that can create income-earning opportunities for the poor. By the same logic, the socially oriented microfinance institutions, which provide financial services to the otherwise underserved poor and are able to cover their operating costs from interest earnings, can qualify as social businesses, as mentioned earlier.

Yet, another way of interpreting the idea of social business in terms of conventional tools of economic analysis is to relate it to the problem of project selection for public-sector investment based on social cost-benefit analysis. Incidentally, by introducing the concept of "accounting" or "shadow pricing" in social cost-benefit analysis, economists have clearly broken away from the stereotype of what Oscar Wilde once described as "someone who knows the price of everything and the value of nothing". This approach to project selection seeks to maximise net social returns from public-sector investment based on *social* costs and benefits which are distinct from private cost-benefit calculations because of taking into account both the problem of economic externalities (by using shadow prices as distinct from market prices) and income distributional considerations (by attaching different social weights to income accruing to different income classes). For example, in the case of a social business catering to the needs of poor consumers, the social returns to the investment may take into account the social value attached to income benefit accruing to the poor consumers (arising from their buying the products at lower than commercially determined prices).

If the consumption of the products entails some public good element, such as health benefits, the social benefits will be even higher. However, while the social cost-benefit analysis is applied to determine the priorities of public-sector investment, the concept of social business belongs entirely to the domain of the market economy driven by private investment. Unlike public-sector projects, a social business has to have a viable (no-loss) business model. Moreover, applying the social cost-benefit approach to assess investment projects for a social business may face the practical problem of getting enough data and information required for such an analysis, particularly because of the innovative nature of such projects.

The risks and pitfalls

The above discussions point to the promise as well as the likely pitfalls of the concept of social business. While the benefits to society are obvious in the case of a successful social business on the grounds discussed above, there are some serious concerns about the difficulties in designing and implementing such a project. One of those concerns has to do with the informational problem that may arise from the fact that a social business may not be able to take full advantage of market signals in making decisions about prices and products. The informational deficiency may arise in perceiving what is good for society while not necessarily maximising profit as allowed by the market. Prices and profits, resulting from self-interested behaviour, serve a useful signalling function since the interests of each person are best known by the person herself or himself. Amartya Sen aptly puts it as, "Doing good is not an easy matter with informational deficiency" (Sen 1984). One has to only recollect O Henry's story "The Gift of the Magi" to see how the pursuit of altruism can lead to frustration. Social businesses, therefore, need to tread between the Scylla of market failures from externalities and the Charybdis of informational deficiency. A safeguard against messing up the market mechanism is, however, provided by the stipulation of running social businesses at least on a no-loss basis, which provides a bottom line for using the market as a disciplining force. Overall, it may be easier to judge the merits of social businesses in particular practical contexts, when the benefits are quite obvious, rather than in terms of any rigorous yardstick of market efficiency or optimality.

The problem of informational deficiency is also linked to business risks. Private capitalists or their financiers take risks while investing in new business ventures. They are willing to undertake the risk of business failure because of the lure of earning profits; in fact, the riskier the investment, the higher are usually the expected returns from profits. Donors and philanthropists, however, may feel less comfortable with the idea that the social businesses they are investing in may in some cases fail to deliver the goods, and they may therefore like to see strict pre-project scrutiny in place. For example, can enough market segmentation be ensured so that the benefits from the products and services intended for the poor do not go to non-poor consumers? Or, given the "public good" characteristics of these products and services, will there be a need for social campaigns to create demand? For example, due to lack of consumer awareness, the nutrition-rich yoghurt produced by Grameen-Danone, mentioned earlier, is alleged to have faced stiff competition from commercially marketed yoghurt of inferior quality.

Moreover, while profits and shareholder dividends are taken as performance yardsticks of profit-motivated businesses, it will be difficult to find one such single measure of success for a social business, so that the performance of each one has to be evaluated in terms of meeting its particular avowed social objectives. As mentioned earlier, a possible approach may be to examine the *social relevance* of the project that may appear obvious in a broader context rather than focusing on any narrowly interpreted impact assessment. How far the social business campaign can create an impact will perhaps depend to a large measure on the resolution of these issues. Motivating the institutions and individuals with enough capital to embrace the idea, of course, remains a more fundamental challenge.

Notes

1 bKash is a subsidiary company of a commercial bank, the BRAC Bank, which in turn was set up by the world-famous NGO, BRAC (stands for Bangladesh Rural Advancement Committee).
2 For a detailed discussion of the growth of the NGO-MFIs in Bangladesh, see Mahmud and Osmani (2017), Chapter 2.

References

Heredia, Ruth. (1997). *The Amul India Story*. New Delhi: Tata McGraw-Hill Publishing Co. Ltd.
Hirsch, F. (1977). *Social Limits to Growth*. London: Routledge and Kegan Paul.
Mahmud, W. and S. R. Osmani. (2017). *The Theory and Practice of Microcredit*. Abingdon, UK: Routledge.
Mills-Scofield, D. (2013). "Every business is (or should be) a social business." *Harvard Business Review*, January 14.
Morishima, M. (1982). *Why Has Japan 'Succeeded'?: Western Technology and Japanese Ethos*. Cambridge, UK: Cambridge University Press.
Piketty, T. (2014). *Capital in the Twenty-First Century*. Cambridge, MA: Harvard University Press.

Sen, Amartya K. (1984). "The profit motive". In Amartya K Sen (ed.), *Resources, Values and Development*, Chapter 3. New Delhi: Oxford University Press.

Winter Jr., S. G. (1969). "A simple remark on the second optimality theorem of welfare economics". *Journal of Economic Theory*, vol. 1, no. 1, pp. 99–103.

World Bank. (2012). *More and Better Jobs in South Asia*. Washington, DC: World Bank.

Yunus, M. (2007). "Social business". Dhaka: Yunus Centre. http://www.muha mmadyunus.org/index.php/social-business/social-business (accessed on March 15, 2017).

Yunus, M. and K. Weber. (2010). *Building Social Business: The New Kind of Capitalism that Serves Humanity's Most Pressing Needs*. New York: Public Affairs.

Index

www.ingramcontent.com/pod-product-compliance
Ingram Content Group UK Ltd.
Pitfield, Milton Keynes, MK11 3LW, UK
UKHW020424010325
455677UK00029B/999